PANZER CREWMAN

SIMON FORTY &
RICHARD CHARLTON-TAYLOR

CASEMATE | ILLUSTRATED

CIS0047

Published in 2025 by
CASEMATE PUBLISHERS
1950 Lawrence Road, Havertown, PA 19083, USA
and
47 Church Street, Barnsley, S70 2AS, UK

Print edition: ISBN 978-1-63624-460-0
Digital edition: ISBN 978-1-63624-461-7

© Simon Forty 2025

Design by Eleanor Forty-Robbins
Printed and bound in the Czech Republic by FINIDR s.r.o.

CASEMATE PUBLISHERS (US)
Telephone (610) 853-9131
Fax (610) 853-9146
Email: casemate@casematepublishers.com
www.casematepublishers.com

CASEMATE PUBLISHERS (UK)
Telephone (0)1226 734350
Email: casemate-uk@casematepublishers.co.uk
www.casematepublishers.co.uk

Author's Note: All photos credited on the captions. The authors thank all those who have contributed, in particular Ruth Sheppard and her team at Casemate for helpful and constructive assistance in squeezing a quart into a pint pot, Eleanor Forty-Robbins (design), Mark Franklin (artwork), Mike Holverson at www.themarshalsbaton.com, Nils Z of MKB, Ian Spring of Pixpast.com, Akira Takiguchi, and Marc Romanych of Digital History for their help with illustrations and other material. If we've omitted anyone in error, please let us know through the publisher. Please note that this book specifically covers the crew of the Panzers, in this case defined as tanks. Crew of other German armored vehicles—*Sturmgeschütze*, *Panzerjäger*, and *Sturmartillerie*—will be covered in a later book.

Title page image: With helmets hanging from the turret *Schürzen*, the crew of this Leibstandarte SS Adolf Hitler command tank watches fall of shot at Kursk in 1943. Note the star aerial and the SS camouflage uniforms. (NARA)
Contents page map: Soviet 1945 map of Berlin. Over 250 tanks were involved in the city's defense in April 1945, including 40 PzKpfw IVs, 30 Panthers, 13 Tiger Is, and 12 Tiger IIs. **A** is the Reichstag and **B** is the Reichs Chancellery complex and the bunker where Hitler killed himself on April 30. (Leningrad Military Mapping Unit/Wikicommons)
Contents page image: In the desert of North Africa, German Panzer crews showed they were streets ahead of the Allies with better training, better tactics, and better tank handling. Here, PzKpfw IIIs are offloaded in an African port. (*Signal*/GF Collection)

Contents

Timeline of Events

Tanks were still new when the Nazis came to power and the world's military theoreticians were still wondering what shape they should take and how best to use them. Within a decade, the German Army would show the world just how important they were in an all-arms approach to warfare that gained them more European territory west of the Urals than any empire ever had before.

1929: The 1922 Treaty of Rapello with the Soviet Union allows Germany to circumvent restrictions imposed by the Treaty of Versailles. The Kama tank school opens in the Soviet Union.

1933: The *Heereswaffenamt* (Army Ordnance Office) issues contracts for a 5-ton AFV. Henschel complete three prototypes in December.

November 1, 1933: *Kraftfahrlehrkommando* (Motorized Training Command) established at Zossen in Germany.

February 3, 1934: Production of the IA LaS (*Landwirtschaftlicher Schlepper*— industrial tractor) that will be designated PzKpfw (MG) (SdKfz 101) Ausf A, the PzKpfw I.

Spring 1935: The first production PzKpfw II enters service.

October 15, 1935: The first three Panzer divisions are formed.

1936: The PzKpfw III and PzKpfw IV enter production.

October 7, 1936: German tanks are sent to Spain to support Franco during the Spanish Civil War.

1937: Henschel instructed to design a *Durchbruchswagen*—breakthrough vehicle—that will lead to the Tiger.

October 1938: Germany occupies the Sudetenland and takes control of Czech military materiel and production. The PzKpfw 35(t) and 38(t) become part of the German inventory.

PzKpfw Is of Guderian's 2. Panzerdivision in Kamenz, Saxony, 1936. It had two tank regiments, Panzerregiment 3 based in Kamenz and 4 in Ohrdruf. (GF Collection)

September 1, 1939: *Fall Weiß.* Just over 3,500 Panzers go into action in the three-pronged attack on Poland. Around 1,000 are lost—although many are recovered and repaired.

May 10, 1940: *Fall Gelb.* Some 2,500 Panzers attack the West. Over half are PzKpfw Is and IIs; the rest are PzKpfw IIIs (349), IVs (280), 35(t)s (118), 38(t)s (207), and PzBefWg (154). They face over 3,000 Allied tanks.

May 20, 1940: Arras counterattack achieves little on the ground, although it contributes to OKH's unease about flank security. They stop the Panzers advancing on Dunkerque.

March 8–10, 1941: *Unternehmen Sonnenblume* sees 5. leichte Division's Panzerregiment 5 land at Tripoli. These are first units of what will become the Deutsches Afrika Korps (DAK).

April 6, 1941: *Unternehmen Marita*, the attack on Greece, and *Weisung 25*, on Yugoslavia, start using just over 850 Panzers in six divisions.

June 22, 1941: *Unternehmen Barbarossa.* Around 3,500 Panzers in 17 divisions divided into four *Panzergruppen* spearhead the invasion of the Soviet Union.

June 23–27, 1941: A huge tank battle takes place at Raseiniai in Lithuania—240 Panzers of Panzergruppe 4 are attacked by 750 Soviet vehicles, including the heavy KV-2s. German victory owes much to effective close-air support.

June 23–30, 1941: Another enormous tank battle, at Brody in Ukraine, sees 750 Panzers of Panzergruppe 1 defeat as many as 3,000 Soviet tanks.

September 30, 1941–January 7, 1942: Attrition caused by combat, the vast distances, and the weather degrade the *Panzertruppen. Unternehmen Taifun*—the attack on Moscow—is beaten back.

April 20, 1942: Hitler's 53rd birthday—Henschel and Porsche demonstrate the capabilities of prototypes of what was to become the most feared tank of the war: the Tiger.

May 17, 1942: The first Tiger—initially named the PzKpfw VI Tiger Ausf H (SdKfz 181)—rolls off the production line. 1,376 are ordered but only chassis numbers 250,001–251,350 are produced.

August 29, 1942: Four Tiger tanks of 1./sPzAbt 502 see action for the first time, on the Leningrad front.

August 30–September 5, 1942: *Unternehmen Brandung*—Rommel tries to finish off British Eighth Army under its new commander, Bernard Montgomery. The important defensive victory of Alam el Halfa is followed up by victory at the second battle of El Alamein, forcing Panzerarmee Afrika into a retreat that ends in Tunisia.

November 1942: Production of the first run of PzKpfw V Panthers—the Ausf D—begins.

January 1943: Henschel receives the formal order for the Tiger II. Production starts in December.

June 23–29, 1943: The Panther is rushed to the battlefield of Kursk. It proves a disastrous initiation because of automotive unreliability.

February 19–23, 1943: Rommel inflicts a sharp defeat on inexperienced American armored troops at Kasserine Pass, Tunisia.

July 5, 1943: The delayed German offensive (*Unternehmen Zitadelle*) at Kursk is launched. The Red Army has had time to set up layered antitank defenses that stand firm.

July 11–12, 1943: A significant tank battle takes place at Prokhorovka. By the time *Zitadelle* is called off, the tide has turned on the Eastern Front.

October 20, 1943: The first Panzerjäger IV is produced. It enters service in January 1944 as the Jagdpanzer IV Ausf F (SdKfz 162). On the same day, the 8.8 cm PaK 43/3 auf Panzerjäger Panther (SdKfz 173) is demonstrated to Hitler. He suggests it should be named Jagdpanther.

November 1943: The PzKpfw VI Tiger Ausf B—the Tiger II—goes into production.

June 6, 1944: The Allies land in Normandy opposed by nine Panzer divisions, but only 21. Panzer is close enough to counter-attack. It carves its way to the coast on June 6 but then retreats. The other divisions are rushed to Normandy, pounded by Allied air, and introduced piecemeal to counter British and Canadian armored thrusts around Caen.

June 8–9, 1944: Elements of the 12. SS-Panzerdivision Hitlerjugend attack the Canadian Regina Rifles at Bretteville l'Orgueilleuse and are repulsed with heavy losses.

July 11, 1944: The Tiger II sees action in the West combating the Canadian Operation *Atlantic*: two are lost.

June 13, 1944: Michael Wittmann attacks the vanguard of British 22nd Armoured Brigade at Villers-Bocage and knocks out 14 tanks. That afternoon, however, the Germans lose six of the 36 Tigers in Normandy, and six PzKpfw IVs.

July 18–20: Operation *Goodwood* sees a huge British armored attack repulsed with some 400 tanks knocked out. A tactical loss, strategically the Germans are forced to keep their armor to the east clearing the way for the American Operation *Cobra*.

July 25–31, 1944: Operation *Cobra* breaks the deadlock in Normandy and punctures the German line. Patton's Third Army sweeps through the gap created by Bradley.

July 26, 1944: Ernst Barkmann of 2. SS-Panzerdivision Das Reich is alleged to have knocked out 15 American tanks in a Panther in just two days.

July 30, 1944: British Operation *Bluecoat* holds German Panzer reinforcements back from closing the *Cobra* breakthrough.

August 1–4, 1944: Battle of Radzymin, the largest tank battle in Poland, sees the destruction of Soviet 3rd Tank Corps by Model.

August 7–13, 1944: *Unternehmen Lüttich*—the Mortain counterattack—sees XLVII. Panzerkorps attempt to cut off the American breakthrough. Its failure results in the creation of the Falaise Pocket.

August 20, 1944: Remaining German Panzer units in Normandy are destroyed trying to escape through the Falaise Gap and in the retreat to the Seine.

August 12, 1944: The Tiger II sees action with sPzAbt 501 during the Lvov–Sandomierz offensive—as many as 14 tanks are lost.

September 8–October 28, 1944: The bloody battles around the Dukla Pass see Heeresgruppe Heinrici's 350 tanks hold off 1,000 from Soviet 1st and 4th Ukrainian Fronts.

September 18–29, 1944: Battle of Arracourt sees U.S. 4th Armored Division defeat attacks by 5. Panzerarmee, helped by American airpower.

December 16, 1944: The last major German assault in Western Europe starts with 6. Panzerarmee attacking through the Ardennes.

October 15, 1944: Essential support for *Unternehmen Panzerfaust* in Budapest is provided by Tiger IIs of sPzAbt 503.

January 1–12, 1945: *Unternehmen Konrad I*, the first of three attempts by IV. SS-Panzerkorps to break through to Budapest. *Konrad II* takes place on January 7–12 and *Konrad III* on January 17–26. All fail.

February 17–14, 1945: *Unternehmen Südwind* clears the Soviet bridgehead over the Hron River preparatory to …

March 6–15, 1945: *Unternehmen Frühlingserwachen*—the last major German offensive—sees I. and II. SS-Panzerkorps fail in their multiple ambitions around Budapest.

April 1945: *Schadpanzer*—some 10 damaged Panthers and 12 PzKpfw IVs from 5. Panzerkompanie (bo)—dig in to help with the defense of Berlin.

May 1, 1945: The last Tiger of Panzerdivision Müncheberg defending Berlin is abandoned on Unter den Linden, near the Brandenburg Gate.

This CAD concept of Das Werk's Borgward IV Panzerjäger Wanze model (kit DW35008) shows the adaptation that was made to 56 of the B IVB and C models (see p. 75) to allow them to play a part in the defense of Berlin in April 1945. Six *Raketenpanzerbüchse 54/1* launchers were attached to the top of the superstructure and three smoke launchers (to cover the vehicle's retreat after firing) to the front. (MKB)

| Abbreviations

APC-HE	armor-piercing (capped)-high explosive
APCBC-HE	armor-piercing, capped, ballistic capped-high explosive
APCR	armor-piercing, composite, rigid (in American parlance HVAP = high velocity armor-piercing)
Ausf	*Ausführung* = equivalent of mark or version
bo	*Bodenständig* = immobile
EK I/II	*Eisernes Kreuz I. Klasse/II. Klasse* = Iron Cross First and Second class
ETO	European Theater of Operations
FuG	*Funkgerät* = radio equipment
GFM	*Generalfeldmarschall* = field marshal
Gr Hl	*Granate KwK Hohlladung* = shaped charge round
HE/HEAT	high explosive/high explosive antitank
HG	*Heeresgruppe* = army group
HiWi	*Hilfswillige* = Eastern European who worked for the German Army (usually the better of two options where the other was dying)
KAN	*Kriegsausrüstungsnachweis* = table of equipment
KE	kinetic energy
Kp	*Kompanie* = company
KStN	*Kreigsstärkenachweisung* = proof of war strength
KwK	*Kampfwagenkanone* = tank gun
L/	*Lauf* = length of gun barrel in calibers
LSSAH	Leibstandarte-SS Adolf Hitler
MAN	Maschinenfabrik Augsburg-Nürnberg
MNH	Maschinenfabrik Niedersachsen-Hannover
Nbgr	*Nebelgranate* = smoke round
nr	*Nummer* = number (no.)
NSKK	*Nationalsozialistisches Kraftfahrkorps* = National Socialist Motor Transport Corps
PaK	*Panzerabwehrkanone* = antitank gun
	Panzerwaffe lit armored weapon = German armored corps
	PzBefWg Panzerbefehlswagen = command tank. Initially, two versions: the kl = *kleiner* = small (PzKpfw I) and gr = *grosse* = large (PzKpfw II)
Pzgr	*Panzergranate* = armor-piercing round
PzKpfw	*Panzerkampfwagen* = tank
RAD	*Reichsarbeitsdienst* = Reich Labor Servce
RAL	*Reichs-Ausschuß für Lieferbedingungen* = National Committee for Delivery Conditions
s(SS)Pz Abt	*schwere (SS-) Panzerabteilung* = heavy tank battalion
SdKfz	*Sonderkraftfahrzeug* = special-purpose vehicle
Sprgr	*Sprenggranate* = HE shell
Stoma	*Stabsoffizier für Marschüberwachung* = staff officer in charge of traffic control
StuG III/IV	*Sturmgeschütz* = assault gun built on either PzKpfw III or IV chassis
(t)	*Tschechoslowakisch* = Czech

Introduction

Analyzing the tactics behind the Blitzkrieg, one thing is obvious. A single element was more powerful than the rest: mobility. Despite the Germans' continued dependence on horsepower and the endurance of its footslogging infantry, it was the far-ranging mobility of the Luftwaffe and Panzerwaffe that spearheaded their attacks. The shock waves of armored thrusts deep into enemy lines, huge encirclement battles, an almost cavalier approach to flank security, and the use of radio communications took the Germans to the brink of complete success. And when you look at the machinery they used, particularly the early Panzers, there was no great technological edge. French and Soviet tanks, even the British Matilda, were more than a match for their German equivalents.

What also set the German Army apart from its counterparts was the teamwork that enabled every level of the Wehrmacht to act on its own initiative, with a highly motivated force that emphasized practicality, leadership, and, of course, ruthlessness. Its attitudes are summed up well in *Panzer Vorwärts!—Aber mit Verstand!* (Armor forward! But with intelligence!), a wartime training booklet with a foreword by Generalinspekteur der Panzertruppen Heinz Guderian (see pp. 114–15). The title alludes to Prussian Field Marshal Gebhardt von Blücher of Waterloo fame, who was nicknamed "*Marschall Vorwärts.*" The booklet combines humor with its messages, each spread juxtaposing a peacetime problem on the left-hand page, with a military principle on the right-hand page. The images are illustrations.

The booklet identified, as its title page outlines, "30 combat principles prepared and summarized by a company commander based on experiences of the campaign against Soviet Russia." It starts by saying:

Panzer—Your weapon! Early poster depicting a commander of the *Panzertruppen* wearing the black Panzer uniform (*Sonderbekleidung der Panzertruppen*) with its rose-pink piping (*Waffenfarbe*) and a skull (*Totenkopf*) on his collar—a traditional symbol used by the hussars from Braunschweig (Brunswick) and Prussia. The problem was that it was also adopted by the SS, as were the black uniforms, and this led to the early demise of many *Panzertruppen* on the Eastern Front where it was assumed they were SS men. The Panzer beret (the M1934 *Schutzmütze*) covered a protective rubber skullcap which was abandoned in early 1941 because it was incompatible for use with headphones. (Wikipedia Commons)

The Panzer regiment is the division's main strike force because of its firepower, armor, and mobility.

Its strength in attack is optimized by surprise, concentration, and ruthlessness.

Responsible leadership and bold use of this powerful force at crucial moments of battle guarantees success.

In 1918 Germany had been soundly defeated by the Allies who had themselves used the embryonic methods of Blitzkrieg—tanks, airpower, artillery, and clever infantry tactics—to force the Germans to capitulate, the Kaiser to abdicate, and Germany itself to be thrown into a turmoil from which the Nazi Party would emerge victorious. Its army was limited by the Treaty of Versailles: it was to have no more than one hundred thousand men with a maximum of four thousand officers, and no more than seven divisions of infantry and three divisions of cavalry

The German response was to set up a clandestine operation to circumvent these strictures. Headed by Generalmajor Hans von Seeckt, the Truppenamt began by analyzing the lessons of the last war. The result was the two-part *Führung und Gefecht der verbundenen Waffen* (*Command and Battle of the Combined Arms*) that appeared in 1921 and 1923—the basis for Blitzkrieg.

Von Seeckt met Hitler in 1923 and later said, "We were one in our aim; only our paths were different." He also said in 1925, "We must become powerful, and as soon as we have power, we will naturally take back everything we have lost." One step toward this was Panzertruppenschule Kama (*Panzertruppenschule* = School for Armored Troops) set up near Kazan in the Soviet Union—a result of the Treaty of Rapallo (1923) where Germany and Russia renounced territorial and financial claims against each other, and the later Berlin Treaty (1926) where Germany and the Soviet Union pledged neutrality if either were attacked. The secret clauses allowed the Germans to train and build weapons in the Soviet Union. To control this, von Seeckt set up *Sondergruppe R* (Special Group *Rußland* = Russia) under Kurt von Schleicher. Other members were Schleicher's adjutant Eugen Ott, future CiC of the Reichswehr Kurt von Hammerstein-Equord, Fedor von Bock and, in the Soviet office, Oskar von Niedermayer.

The training in Russia lasted until the Nazis came to power and brazenly renounced Versailles in 1935, increasing the Wehrmacht by bringing in conscription. The 100,000-strong cadre of 1933 had swollen to over 3.7 million in 1939. This expansion was supposed to continue until 1941 when war would be on the cards: unfortunately for the German army, Hitler didn't stick to the timetable.

The new recruits came from an increasingly militarized society—very different to the Western Allies, for whom the legacy of the Great War was the promotion of pacifism, appeasement, and a sincere desire not to do anything that would lead to war; attitudes that would allow Hitler to march into the Rhineland in 1936, Austria in March 1938, the Sudetenland in October 1938, and the rest of Czechoslovakia in 1939.

During this period, German industry had started producing the weapons it would need for war. There were problems. The creation of the Luftwaffe had taken up significant amounts of capital, manpower, industrial commitment, and raw materials. Investment in the Panzerwaffe had seemed as if it would also be substantial: on September 27, 1935, the Kommando der Panzertruppen (Armored Troops Command) was created. Shortly after, on October 15, the first three Panzer divisions were set up at Weimar, Würzburg, and Berlin. The plan was that by 1941 these divisions, three light divisions, and 44 more Panzer battalions would be equipped with nearly two thousand PzKpfw IIIs and IVs, as well as the lighter PzKpfw Is and IIs being built. But these figures hide the fact that the army budgets were skewed more towards guns—particularly artillery—rather than tanks and motor vehicles. There were still doubts about tanks in the military establishment in Germany, as there were in the rest of the world. The Panzerwaffe was still untried, and the use of tanks in the Spanish Civil War did not lead to any strong conclusions as to how it would best be employed in a future war. The naval expansion plan approved in 1939 was given priority over all other industrial projects. Ultimately, the naval plan and all the other commitments led to a reduction in Panzer production by half, something that the acquisition of Austria, the Sudetenland, and Czechoslovakia could hide as those countries' reserves entered the Reich's coffers and the PzKpfw 35(t)s and 38(t)s rolled off the Czech production lines straight into the Panzer divisions. They needed them. On September 1, 1939, there were only 98 PzKpfw IIIs and 211 PzKpfw IVs available for use.

German tank production started slowly, and it was only in 1944 that it hit its peak—and that despite the attentions of the Allied air forces. These factors—along with decision-making processes that led to the range of vehicles and the difficulties with raw materials at the end of the war—meant that Germany produced fewer armored vehicles during the war years than might be expected. The Germans could be accused of complacency because of the ease of the victories. They were probably guilty of taking their foot off the gas because they thought they'd won. Indeed, after the fall of France, Hitler decided to disband 35 of the army's 155 divisions.

The campaigns of 1939 and 1940 took their toll on the Panzer divisions. At the forefront of the action, it's often forgotten that both campaigns were hard fought. Nevertheless, there were sufficient replacements for both vehicles and crew and Hitler rescinded his disbandment order, deciding instead that relations with the Soviet Union were deteriorating

The all-arms approach was key to Blitzkrieg. Tanks needed to be supported by air and artillery and, of course, infantry. The trouble was that during *Barbarossa* the tanks advanced so far, so quickly, that the infantry couldn't keep up. The German Army was a horse-drawn army and its infantry, for the most part, marched on foot. The great *Kesselschlachten* (cauldron battles) of encirclement in 1941 saw the German tanks having to fight defensive battles against Soviets trying to get out of the *Kessel* and those trying to help them from the outside. Unsurprisingly, the *Kessel* were more porous than they should have been, which contributed to continued Soviet resistance. (GF Collection)

Panzer Production to End 1940

Type	To 1938	1938–end 1940
PzKpfw I	1,493	No additions
PzKpfw II	332	1,157
PzKpfw 35(t)	219 (acquired by conquest)	
PzKpfw 38(t)		520 (company acquired by conquest)
PzKpfw III	38	1,140
PzKpfw IV	13	521
Kl PzBefWg	190	No additions
Gr PzBefWg	–	104
Total	**2,285**	**3,442**

German tank production stuttered in the early war years. However, as the fighting on the Eastern Front intensified, so did tank construction, but it was curtailed by Allied bombing. The production target of tanks for MAN (Maschinenfabrik Augsburg-Nürnberg) failed to achieve the 600-unit target it had been ordered to produce by early 1943. It also led to an extreme shortage of spare parts which didn't help maintenance units in the field. (Narodowe Archiwum Cyfrowe [NAC Polish Archives])

enough to warrant the immediate planning for *Barbarossa* to be brought to the fore. Having made this decision, the Panzerwaffe was expanded rapidly, with 10 new Panzer divisions (11–20) being raised between August 1, 1940 and January 10, 1941.

Between the fall of France and the start of *Barbarossa*, the Panzers were involved in *Marita* in the Balkans and Greece, and *Sonnenblume*, the support of Italian forces in the North African desert. Crews and vehicles had to cope with severe terrain (mountains during *Marita* and, of course, the desert heat and sand in *Sonnenblume*). While the total write-offs in the former were few (9 PzKpfw Is, 13 PzKpfw IIs, PzKpfw 38(t)s, 21 PzKpfw IIIs, and 8 PzKpfw IVs), 2. Panzerdivision's Panzerregiment 3 losses could have been a lot worse had the first voyage of the freighters *Marburg* and *Kybels* taking the regiment's tanks from Patras in Greece to Taranto in Italy hit the mines laid by HMS *Abdiel*. In fact, the freighters returned to Patras and were reloaded—mainly with artillery weapons and vehicles—for the next trip, during which they hit the mines. Both freighters sank on May 19, 1941.

Another shipping incident saw Panzerregiment 5, loading at Naples as part of 5. leichte Division bound for North Africa, lose ten PzKpfw IIs and three PzKpfw IVs as the vessel they were loaded on, the *Leverkusen*, caught fire and sank. It was an inauspicious start to a campaign that would drag on until 1943. A sideshow to the main event in the Soviet Union, the Panzers of the Afrika Korps and its descendent units—Panzerarmee Afrika and, ultimately, Heeresgruppe Afrika—fought with distinction in the desert. As an example of how the Panzers showed up the tactical weaknesses of British armor, one need look no further than the fighting between May 26 and July 20, 1942, at Gazala and the Ruweisat Ridge when the 15. and 21. Panzerdivisionen claimed 1,388 British tanks (the actual write-off figure was less than that; the RAOC recovered 581 tanks up to June 19, repaired 278 of them, and sent 222 back to Egypt for repair) for a loss of 233 unrepairable Panzers. The brilliance of the DAK, however, was blunted by the 1st South African and 18th Indian Brigades, and lack of fuel forced the Germans to retreat.

The decisive battle of the desert war saw the preponderance of Allied forces finally break through the Axis defensive layers at El Alamein. Panzerregimenter 5 and 8 opened the battle on October 23, 1942, with 128 and 111 Panzers operational; by November 2 that had dwindled to 75 and 56 respectively. On December 2, the combined operational Panzer strength for Panzerarmee Afrika was 53. The Germans rushed reinforcements across to Tunisia where Allied landings had taken place in November 1942. The reinforcements included 90. leichte and 10. Panzerdivisionen and Army sPzAbt 501, the first Tiger unit in Africa—a combined total of 28 PzKpfw IIs, 182 PzKpfw IIIs, 30 PzKpfw IVs, 11 PzBefWgs, and 20 Tigers. They were joined by sPzAbt 504 in March 1943 (11 Tigers and 19 PzKpfw IIIs), a *Kampfgruppe* (battle group) from Pz-Div Hermann Göring (2 PzKpw IIIs and 8 PzKpfw IVs), and a further 52 PzKpfw IIs and 142 PzKpfw IVs. But the reinforcements were too little, too late. The Panzers had proven their prowess to the U.S. Army at Kasserine at the end of February but couldn't stop the Allied advance on Tunis. In the end, on May 4, a few days before the Axis forces surrendered, only 44 PzKpfw IIIs, 25 PzKpfw IVs, and a single Tiger were still operational.

From the Arctic to the Med, Panzer crew had to cope with very varied terrain and climates. These two photographs show very different locations. This (**below left**) is a PzKpfw III Ausf H of Panzerabteilung 40 in Finland advancing toward the frontline at the start of *Unternehmen Polarfuchs* on July 1, 1941, in an attempt to block the rail route to Murmansk. The other (**below right**) shows PzKpfw IV Ausf G tanks from II. Panzerabteilung Rhodos, on Rhodes in the Dodecanese, August 1943. (SA-Kuva; NAC)

Panzers Deployed on June 22, 1941

I	II	35(t)	38(t)	III	IV	PzBefWg	Total
337	890	155	625	973	439	225	3,644

While the Afrika Korps was attaining almost mythic status in the sands of North Afrika, the Wehrmacht was similarly flattering to deceive in the East. *Barbarossa* opened with seventeen Panzer divisions in four *Panzergruppen* spearheading the assault on the Soviet Union.

The four *Panzergruppen* were commanded by Generalobersts Erich Hoepner (PzGruppe 4, HG Nord; 1., 6., and 8. Panzerdivisionen), Hermann Hoth (PzGruppe 3, HG Mitte; 7., 12., 19., and 20. Panzerdivisionen), Heinz Guderian (PzGruppe 2, HG Mitte; 3., 4., 10., 17., and 18. Panzerdivisionen), and Paul Ludwig Ewald von Kleist (PzGruppe 1, HG Süd; 9., 11., 13., 14., and 16. Panzerdivisionen).

As the Panzers thrust forward and huge encirclement battles trapped enormous numbers of Soviet soldiers, they thought they had achieved what they had in the West—complete victory. But the Soviets didn't give up. Huge casualties, huge losses of materiel, and huge losses of territory didn't stop them from resisting strongly and counterattacking whenever they could. And the tanks they had in their arsenal sent shivers down German spines: the KVs were huge and German shells bounced off them. The T-34s, with their sloping armor, were a surprise that forced the Germans to field improved antitank guns.

Then the Russian climate came into play: first the *rasputitsa* (muddy season of rains) when nothing could move save for *Panjewagen* (horse carts); then the coldest winter for many years, for which the Germans hadn't received cold-weather clothing.

The German thrusts towards Moscow failed. Hitler's Directive 39 put the *Ostheer* (Army of the East) onto a defensive footing. At that moment, the Soviets counterattacked and forced the German Army to give up territory, engendered panic in some units, and cost Guderian his position after he refused to enforce Hitler's famous December 20 order forbidding withdrawals.

To help matters in the East, five new Panzer divisions (20., 21., 22., 23., 24., and 25.) were created between August 1, 1941 and February 28, 1942 (there would be two more in September and October 1942, 26. and 27.), a number of *SS-Panzerabteilungen* were created (one each for LSSAH, Wiking, Das Reich, and Totenkopf; only Wiking's SS-Abteilung 5 saw action before 1943), and the four *Panzergruppen* became Panzerarmeen: 1. (von Kleist) on October 6, 1941; 2. (Guderian) on October 5, 1941; 3. (Reinhardt—having taken over from Hoth on October 5, 1941) on January 1, 1942; 4. On January 1, 1942, command switched from Hoepner to Hoth.

This rebuilding was urgently needed. By March 5, 1942, the 257th day of the Russian campaign, the Germans had sustained over a million casualties (excluding medical casualties which were around 300,000) including over 210,000 dead. By June that figure had reached two million (including 715,000 sick). Around 200,000 horses had died.[1] Over 3,000 tanks had been

Winter Problems

Entries from Halder's diary[2] around this period highlight the problems faced by men, animals, and machines:

10 November 1941

Special winter equipment cannot be brought to Heeresgruppe Süd before Jan.; in some sectors of Heeresgruppe Mitte arrival may be delayed even until late Jan.

18 November 1941

Truck position: Of 500,000 trucks, 150,000 are total losses. 60,000 new trucks will have come off production by Apr. 42. The deficit of 90,000 trucks must be made up through organizational changes; 275,000 trucks must be repaired. For this we need 300,000 tons of spare parts.

27 November 1941

Gen Wagner reports: We are at the end of resources in both personnel and materiel. We are about to be confronted with the dangers of deep winter. Provision for a sudden break of the weather must be made before middle of January. Situation particularly difficult north of Moscow. ... Horses: situation very serious. Distressing lack of forage. Horses must be dispersed over larger areas.

6 December 1941

North: ... Very severe cold (38° below freezing), numerous cases of death from cold. ... Situation aggravated by the cold (30 to 35° of frost). Out of five tanks only one was able to fire. Snowfall now would neutralize our tanks.

9 December 1941

Horses: 1,100 dead daily. By April one quarter of our horse strength will be removed. Requirement 160,000. Requisition 85,000 now plus additional 85,000. Must be at the front when spring operations begin. ... Guderian reports that the condition of his troops is so critical that he does not know how to fend off the enemy. ... He is scraping together in the rear whatever forces he can get hold of in one Armd Div 1,600 rifles!; tank gunners and drivers of course not used as infantry. [Halder was wrong; they were. Sander of Panzerregiment 11 recorded in his diary[3] on November 29, 1941: "Panzer soldiers have turned into infantrymen. We are to be deployed as a protection battalion ... The men of the Panzerregiment are to form an infantry battalion."]

13 December 1941

Report on inspection of troops in Heeresgruppe Mitte. Morale good. One-third of trucks immobilized by mechanical defects. Winter clothing has arrived but materiel for cold-weather operation of vehicles (winter oil etc.) is still outstanding.

14 December 1941

Train arrivals have dropped to an alarming low. The reason given is demolitions by partisans. Railroad repair shop at Velikie Luki burnt down.

5 February 1942

Generaloberarzt Dr Handloser; a) Report on medical casualties. Total in the Armies of the East 60,000, plus 977 officers. b) Typhus: 4,400 cases, 729 fatal.

permanently lost. Three Panzer divisions (6., 7., and 10.) as well as the SS-Das Reich division were withdrawn to the West for rebuilding. Hitler had decided that in 1942 the German Army should secure the oilfields in the Caucasus, and so there was a general reorganization and rebuilding to beef up HG Süd in time for its offensive. Part of this included moving 4. Panzerarmee to HG Süd. The Panzer divisions in HGs Nord and Mitte were reduced to a single battalion. By the beginning of July, the northern divisions averaged around 65 to 70 Panzers each. In the south, the figure was nearer 150 and the total for HG Süd at the start of *Fall Blau* was 1,934 tanks and StuGs.

The results of the eventual attack into the Caucasus were as brilliant as those in 1941. The Panzers advanced deep into the south: Belgorod fell, then Voronezh, Maikop, Novorossisk, and by mid-November 1942, 90 percent of Stalingrad was in German hands.

Once again, victory slipped from German fingertips. Three months later, on February 2, 1943, what was left of 6. Armee surrendered at Stalingrad. It had held out long enough for the troops in the Caucasus to retreat to safety through a narrow corridor around Rostov.

The massive initial successes of *Fall Blau* were hard won. At the end of the first week (June 28 to July 5, 1942) 4. Panzerarmee had only 435 Panzers operational from an initial strength of 633. By November, the Panzer divisions along the Stalingrad axis were dealing with significant losses and were running at 30–40 percent of their authorized strength (*Sollstärke*). This attrition contributed to a dramatic change of the German Army's position at the beginning of 1943, when in Russia Stalingrad fell and, in the Mediterranean, Tunisia.

The Soviet counterattack, Operation *Uranus*, saw 6. Armee surrounded, and further extended by Operation *Little Saturn*, Soviet forces threatened to cut off German troops in the Caucasus. This forced the Germans to regroup. HG Don, under GFM Erich von Manstein, was created and tasked with rescuing 6. Armee. It failed. Though it got within 31 miles/50 kilometers, Manstein's counterattack cut off the Soviet thrust to the Dnieper,

The opening months of *Barbarossa* saw the *Panzertruppen* leading the way through the border defenses and penetrating deeply into the Red Army's rear areas. Huge *Kesselschlachten* took place, this one near Bialystok-Wolkowysk (today, Vawkavysk in Belarus) between June 22–27, 1941. This is better known today as the battle of Bialystok–Minsk in which Guderian's 2. and Hoth's 4. Panzergruppen surrounded around 450,000 men from four Soviet armies, of whom at least 340,000 were killed, wounded, or captured. The Germans lost over 12,000 men and around 100 tanks. (NARA)

The Panzer Situation in 1942[4]

Panzers	Lost by end of 1941	Reinforcements & replacements	Total Ostheer, Jan. 1942	Total Ostheer, July 1942	Total German stock, July 1942
PzKpfw I	428	12	0	0	692
PzKpfw II	424	201	667	410	1,021
PzKpfw 35/38(t)	796	108	92	322	471
PzKpfw III	660	558	921	1,271	2,604
PzKpfw IV	348	140	231	369	723
PzBefWg	79	25	171	65	266
StuG	104	117	272	399	780
	2,839[5]	1,161	2,354[6]	2,836[7]	6,557

retook Kharkov, and reestablished a strong German defensive line. Manstein was helped by the arrival of reinforcements between December 1942 and June 1943 that included, from the West, 6. and 7. Panzerdivisionen, the SS-PzGr-Divisionen LSSAH, Das Reich, and Totenkopf; from HG Mitte, 11., 17., and 19. Panzerdivisionen, Inf-Div (mot.) Großdeutschland; from HG A 3. and 23. Panzerdivisionen and SS-PzGr-Division Wiking; and several Panzer and StuG battalions, including the Tigers of sPzAbt 503. On March 10, 1943, this gave a Panzer strength of 491 in southern Russia.

Manstein, after retaking Kharkov, wanted to push on towards Kursk creating a southern pincer. HG Mitte would supply the northern arm. Had he been able to continue, the battle of Kursk might have been different. As it was, the *rasputitsa*, troop exhaustion, and apathy in HG Mitte, led to a hiatus. The result was that *Unternehmen Zitadelle* didn't take place till July. The plus was that the Panzer force had increased to 2,462,[8] including the latest Panzer, the PzKpfw V Panther, whose arrival promised so much. The downside was that the Soviets had had time to prepare their defenses.

The breathing space provided by Manstein's Panzers gave the Germans one final opportunity to wrest back the initiative and deal the Soviets a suitably significant reverse. *Unternehmen Zitadelle*—the battle of Kursk—didn't deliver. Instead, it wasted men and materiel that could have been better used in the defense. While it is unlikely that moving immediately to a defensive position would have been able to stem the Soviet attacks for any great length of time, especially after the Allies invaded in the West to make it a war on three European land fronts, it may have been possible to stave off the inevitable for rather longer. The collapse of the Eastern Front after Kursk would see that, by August 1944, the Soviet armies had retaken the territory that they had lost in 1941.

By this time, Guderian had come back into the picture as *General-Inspekteur der Panzertruppen* (Inspector-General of Armored Troops); he argued against Kursk but to no avail. The result was a severe mauling for both sides—but the Soviets could better take it. The

After the success of *Barbarossa* in 1941, the reversals that followed the failure to defeat the Red Army saw a more pragmatic Panzerwaffe in 1942. Beefed up with men and vehicles to make up for the considerable losses it had taken in 1941, there would be great successes as the southern element of *Fall Blau* took the Panzers all the way into the Caucasus. In the northern area, 4. Panzerarmee sped toward the outskirts of Voronezh, and while they took the west of the city they were unable conquer all of it. Here a German SdKfz 251 Ausf C—produced to be the mainstay of the *Panzergrenadiere* as there just weren't enough Hanomags to meet demand—is on its way to Voronezh past a well-camouflaged truck, July 1942. (NAC)

Germans, as was usually the case, had the better of the kill:loss ratios. Christopher A. Lawrence gives figures of 2,471 Soviet tanks and 1,536 German tanks destroyed, damaged, and broken down.[9] These figures include the tank destroyers and assault guns of both sides. He argues persuasively that many other assessments of the battle tend to compare apples with oranges, for example not including German command tanks, and not realizing that such was the wealth of Soviet resources, they could afford to write off vehicles the Germans would have had to repair.

In the end, the statistics are less important than the result: after Kursk, the Ostheer spent the rest of the war retreating. The Panzers gave a remarkable account of themselves but could not stop the inevitable. The Soviets in general, and especially their armor, had gained the initiative, learned how to beat the Germans, and did so with increasing proficiency.

The Western Allies had a similar learning curve. In Sicily, the Germans gave a masterly example of trading space for time; they did the same on the mainland. To be fair, the Allies' heart wasn't in the Italian campaign. The Americans thought it a waste of time and once Italy had been knocked out of the war and Rome had fallen, didn't contribute sufficiently to help force the issue. They didn't need to. After the invasion of Normandy, with the Soviet armies across the Dnieper, the end was never in doubt.

In Normandy, the Panzers performed heroically against an opponent that, in the first days, had massive naval gun support, and throughout the campaign complete air supremacy. Continuously inserted into the battle as they became available, they were able to contain British and Canadian thrusts towards Caen, and after it fell, farther south for two months. They were never able to put a sufficient concentration of Panzer divisions together to land a blow against the Allies and had to be content in propaganda victories—such as Wittmann at Villers-Bocage or the carnage of Operation *Charnwood*. When at last they did attempt an armored counterattack—*Unternehmen Lüttich*—to contain the American breakout in the West, all they managed to do was create a salient that devolved into the Falaise Pocket. And while they managed to save more men and equipment than they were expected to have done, they were chased helter-skelter back to the borders of the Reich where they were able to cobble together a defense that owed more to the Allies' fuel problems than anything else.

The most serious tank battle in this period was at Arracourt, where 262 German tanks and StuGs—elements of 5. Panzerarmee—counterattacked U.S. Third Army in Lorraine. By this time the American tankers knew what they were doing. What's more, they faced an enemy who—although equipped with many new Panthers and including veterans of 11. Panzerdivision—included many poorly trained recruits. American airpower was also greatly in evidence. The result was the sort of battle the Germans were accustomed to, but from the other side. Clever tactics and excellent gunnery stopped the German attack and saw 86 Panzers destroyed and 114 more out of action. Only 62 were operational by the battle's end compared to American losses of 25 tanks and 7 tank destroyers.

There would be further tank battles in the future, most notably in the futile Ardennes counteroffensive, Hitler's brainchild that after initial successes—mainly caused by the shock of the attack to troops who were still recovering from the heavy fighting in the Hürtgen Forest—failed to deliver any more than the opportunity for the Allies to destroy more of the German armor and, more importantly, more of their dwindling number of first-class *Panzertruppen*. In the West, after the Ardennes, there would be heavy fighting in Reichswald and crossing the Rhineland, but the war was lost. Before the Ardennes campaign, Panzers available in the West were:[10]

Type	Available	Operational
PzKpfw IV	503	391
Panther	471	336
Tiger I/II	123	79
Totals	1,097	806

The power of propaganda. The battle of Villers-Bocage shows how legends are made. The devastation of advance elements of the Desert Rats was picked on by SS propagandists and helped promote the thesis that German tanks and tankers were a cut above the rest. There is undoubtedly some truth in this. Michael Wittmann, who was acclaimed as having stopped the British 7th Armoured Division single-handedly, caught them with their pants down. However, what the propaganda omits is that the attack was not just by Wittmann—although his part in it was significant—as well as that the subsequent fighting in the town saw the Germans lose around fifteen tanks, including six precious sSS-PzAbt 101 Tigers. This photo shows Tiger 112 of SS-Oberscharführer Heinrich Ernst and a Panzer Lehr PzKpfw IV knocked out by antitank guns of C Company, 1/7 Queen's Royal Regiment. (GF Collection)

Above: Morale is a tenuous thing. At the start of the war, German soldiers had it in spades; by 1942 they had begun to tire. The size of the Soviet Union, the bitter fighting and mounting death toll, and the lice and hard living led to a grim determination to see things through to the bitter end. The German soldiers still believed in their cause and their leaders, but fatalism set in. As the Allies found when they brought in replacements, there were tensions between the hardened old-timers—*Ostkämpfer*—and new men replacing the old timers' dead friends. As Ganz says in *Ghost Division*, "While some were returning wounded combat veterans ... perhaps 30 percent were '*Neulinge*' [novices]." An added factor was that divisions had recruited in a *Wehrkreis*, meaning they all came from the same area—in the case of Ganz's 11. Panzerdivision, Silesia. The *Neulinge* came from all over Germany and had different accents and a different outlook—especially as the Red Army neared and then fought over Silesia itself. What did help was "that the unit commanders and many junior Offiziere and Unteroffiziere had risen within the division and gave it cohesion." Here a tank crew poses for *Kriegsberichter* Tissen with their big-eared mascot. (NARA)

By March 15, 1945, after battle attrition and the movement of units to the East, this had shrunk to:

Type	Available	Operational
PzKpfw IV	59	19
Panther	152	49
Tiger	28	6
Totals	239	74

All told, there were around 200 Panzers in Italy.

In the East, no matter how hard the High Command parroted the need to stand and fight, no matter how many *Festungen* (fortresses) were declared, there was little the Ostheer could do to stem the tide. On May 31, 1944, the army was still functioning. It was retreating and had suffered large casualties, but German industry was producing more vehicles than at any time of the other war. The number of operational Panzers on the Eastern Front was:

Type	Available	Operational
PzKpfw IV	603	484
Panther	313	238
Tiger	298	233
Totals	1,214	955

Surprisingly, although the borders had shrunk, on March 15, 1945, the availability was very similar:

Type	Available	Operational
PzKpfw IV	603	314
Panther	776	387
Tiger	212	125
Totals	1,591	826

However, many Panzers were bottled up in Kurland or were fighting their way back through Hungary and Austria to be able to surrender in the West rather than the East. The Red Army had the initiative, the strength, and the skills to win, and apart from a few tactical reverses in Hungary and a few counterattacks in Poland and East Germany, it was all over bar the shouting.

Left: On December 4, 1941, Moscow was within reach but the thermometer read –37°C (–34.6°F). All the winter clothing that most soldiers had, as this winter scene shows, was the standard greatcoat and, if they were lucky, a Russian hat. Anyone who spent too much time outside got frostbitten; everyone learnt to check their buddies to stop it from happening. The tanks had trouble turning their engines over, the optics fogged up, and the breechblocks wouldn't open. The freezing German soldiers scavenged cold-weather gear from dead Soviet soldiers, particularly their felt boots. The Panzers were only heated by the engines—and when they froze, the best way to warm them up was to pour petrol into a ration tin filled with earth and ignite it. One tin went under the engine, another under the differential. Alternatively, running the engines for 10–15 minutes every hour helped but didn't stop frost accumulating inside the tank. This frost caused shorts in wiring as it thawed. On top of all that, the fighting continued unabated. (NAC)

The Soldier

After the Treaty of Versailles, the Imperial German Army's General Staff went underground and became the Truppenamt under Generalmajor Hans von Seeckt, who set up committees to examine the lessons of the recent war. This led to vigorous debate by junior officers who went on to develop the two-part *Führung und Gefecht der verbundenen Waffen* (*Command and Battle of the Combined Arms*) that appeared in 1921 and 1923—the rulebook for the tactics that shocked the world between 1939 and 1941.

Training

Von Seeckt's new systems led to intensive training. As there was such a small officer base, this training also concentrated on the NCOs, ensuring that each could not only do his own job but that of the next level above. The new army was, in reality, a training cadre that—when the time was right—would be able to expand quickly and train new recruits.

Part of the subterfuge included a deal with the Soviet Union. In 1929 the Kama tank school (*Panzerschule/Kampfwagenschule*) opened on the Volga River near Kazan in the Soviet Union. A secret training school run by the German military, Germans and Russians trained there as tank drivers, radio operators, and gunners, and were given tactical training. As well as German Army staff, Krupp and Rheinmetall supplied technicians and engineers, as well as "agricultural machinery"—a codename for various vehicles: two Rheinmetall 16-ton vehicles

The Light Tractor (*Leichttraktor*) was one of three types of experimental tank secretly tested in Russia at the Kama testing grounds. The name "Light Tractor" was a cover to avoid sanctions imposed by the Treaty of Versailles after World War I. These tractors provided valuable insights for future tank production and were used for training purposes pre- and early war, returning from the Soviet Union once the Nazis came to power. (Via Swedish Tank Archives [http://tanks.mod16.org])

Entry of the armored car troops into their new home at Wünsdorf on October 20, 1935. The march past the guests of honor is at the site boundary on the Chaussee Zossen–Baruth. The first Panzer—a kleiner Befehlswagen based on the PzKpfw I Ausf A chassis—is about to break through a ribbon which has been stretched across the road. (Bundesarchiv_Bild_183-2006-1023-500)

with 7.5 cm guns; six heavy tractors, two each from Rheinmetall, Krupp, and Daimler—arrived later in 1929; and Rheinmetall lightweight tractors. These had a rotating turret that had a 3.7 cm gun, then a machine gun that arrived in 1930. Among the officers who trained, instructed, or visited Kama, were many destined for important roles in the war such as Werner von Blomberg, Walter Model, Wilhelm Ritter von Thoma, and Heinz Guderian.

After the Nazis gained power in 1933, the Kama school was closed, and on September 15 the vehicles were returned to Germany. They went to the gunnery school at Putlos via Leningrad and Szczecin.

After 1933 and the Nazi takeover, life for young men in the Reich became increasingly militarized. The Hitlerjugend instilled a fighting spirit and concentrated on fitness and ideological indoctrination. This was continued by compulsory service in the Reichsarbeitsdienst (RAD). All this meant that most young men entering the Wehrmacht had already had the equivalent of basic military training, were in excellent physical condition, and had been indoctrinated both with Nazi ideology and military attitudes.

After a period of basic training ranging from 12 to 16 weeks, tank crew went for specialist training at the *Panzertruppenschule*. The first Panzer crew training unit in Germany—Kraftfahrlehrkommando Zossen—was set up in November 1933 at Wünsdorf-Zossen, south of Berlin. It became the *Kraftfahrkampftruppenschule* (Motor Troop Combat School)

Before the arrival of training vehicles, wooden mockups were used. (Via Leo Marriott)

The PzKpfw I Ausf B *ohne Ausbau* (without a superstructure) was originally planned for use as a recovery vehicle but proved too small to do this. It ended up being used mainly for driver training, as here, a Fahrschulpanzer I (driving-school tank). Most of this training was at NSKK schools. (GF Collection)

in 1936 and the *Panzertruppenschule* (Armored Troop School) in 1937. It was later (in 1941) renamed Panzertruppenschule I and moved to Bergen-Belsen, which had bigger training grounds. It was renamed for the final time in 1944, when it became Panzertruppenschule Bergen. It trained tank crew and antitank personnel.[12]

Panzertruppenschule II was so named in 1943 having evolved from the *Schule für Schnelle Truppen* (School for Mobile Troops) which had been created in 1941 at the old cavalry school at Potsdam-Krampnitz, where Panzergrenadiers and tank reconnaissance troops were trained. They used training grounds at the famous *Truppenübungsplatz* (military training area) Döberitz. Late in 1944, the two *Panzertruppenschulen* merged.

Both *Panzertruppenschulen* had elements in other locations. For example, *Panzerjäger* (tank destroyer) courses at Sülze/Evensen south of Hanover and *Panzeraufklärung* (reconnaissance) courses at Beckedorf to the west of Hannover. Other specialist schools were also set up, such as in Paris (*Abteilungsführerschule*—School for Battalion Leaders) and Versailles (*Kompanieführerschule*—company leaders) both in 1942, and a Panzerjäger school at Mielau/Grafenwöhr and *Panzeraufklärung* courses at Lutschientz, both in 1944.

Other specialist courses were introduced for training crew to use the PzKpfw V Panther (at Erlangen) and PzKpfw VI Tiger (Paderborn). Setting up this training wasn't always straightforward because of the exigencies of war: the first Panther

A Fahrschulpanzer I in the snow. These driving-school tanks were nicknamed *Fahrschulwanne*, where *Wanne* is a corruption of *Badwanne* (meaning bathtub). (SF Collection)

Another *Fahrschulpanzer III* based on a PzKpfw III Ausf A chassis. The first version of the PzKpfw III had only five wheels and entered service in 1937. The suspension wasn't fit for purpose and the armor was too easily penetrated, so they were taken out of combat service and used as driver trainers. (GF Collection)

training units had to spend more time ironing out technical problems and as the war went on, Guderian made changes to the program to speed up the deployment of Panther crews, cutting training times and emphasizing gunnery above all else.

The main army shooting training took place at the *Schießschule der Panzertruppen* (Armored Troop Gunnery School) Putlos, northwest of Oldenburg in Holstein on the Baltic. It originated in 1935. The students sent to Putlos undertook live-fire exercises, and night and dusk training missions.

There were several different types of officer and NCO schools for armored troops:

- *Fahnenjunkerschulen der Panzertruppe* for officer aspirants (*Offizieranwärter*—OAs. From October 1942, these were distinguished with a double-braid loop around their shoulderstraps).

- *Oberfähnrichschulen der Panzertruppe* for those who had passed the OA course. Most served a term of probation in the field and were then commissioned.

- *Heeresunteroffizersschulen der Panzertruppe* for NCOs, the main center from September 1942 being at Rembertow (today, Rembertów) east of Warsaw where there was a 12-week course. The school moved to Wischau (today's Vyskov in Czechia) in mid-1944 and then again in 1945 to Wildflecken in Bavaria.

Advanced enlisted men could be selected as officer candidates and would then attend a military academy (before the war there were four *Kriegsschulen*, at Potsdam, Dresden, Hannover, and München).

Halfway through the *Lehrgang* (course of instruction), the *Fahnenjunker* (or *Offizieranwärter*, officer candidate) became a *Fähnrich* (cadet), and then an *Oberfähnrich*. Later, if successful, he'd be promoted to *Leutnant* (lieutenant). Once the course had been completed, they joined the rest of the troops in a *Panzerersatzabteilung* (Tank Replacement Battalion) attached to a Panzer division. There were also special service branch schools, and the program was expanded during the war.[13]

Driver training was mainly undertaken by instructors from the NSKK. A turretless version of the PzKpfw I was used for driving and maintenance training. Under the guise of motor sport, the NSKK trained many who would go on to become Panzer drivers and mechanics. Initial driver training was given using cutdown examples of the Panzer I or Panzer I with the turret and superstructure removed.

During the interwar period, most armies undertook maneuvers—the U.S. Army's Louisiana Maneuvers being the best known—but the Germans were conducting huge training exercises involving multiple divisions, as in Hesse, September 21–25, 1936, when fifty thousand men were involved. Another such example of this were the "Mussolini" maneuvers, the final event of which took place in front of Il Duce (among others, including the British CIGS) on September 26, 1937. The maneuvers proper were held at Mecklenburg on September 18–24, 1937. They involved 160,000 men, 830 tanks, 21,000 vehicles, and 25,000 horses, and its week of exercises involved aircraft, eight infantry divisions, 3. Panzerdivision, 1. Panzerbrigade (Panzerregimenter 1 and 2), seven antiaircraft battalions, and six reconnaissance squadrons. They were realistic, too: "the strain on all participating commanders was probably as close to actual war as any exercise has ever been."[13] Most important, they showed that German armored divisions were sufficiently trained and equipped to be capable of independent action—this was thanks to the participation of 3. Panzerdivision, which decided the "Red" side's success against the "Blues."

This extensive prewar training ensured the tank crews of 1939 understood the all-arms tactics that were the hallmarks of what we call Blitzkrieg. With close-air support a major factor, the successes of the German campaigns of 1939–41 show how extensive and effective this training had been. Hermann Balck opined:[14]

> During World War II the operational training of the German Wehrmacht reached a peak unsurpassed by any other army at any other time. That was to the credit of Seeckt, who by building on Schlieffen's ideas administered that legacy in a masterful way. … No other army has managed to achieve what the thirty-six hundred-strong officer corps of the one hundred-thousand-man army accomplished during World War II in

PzKpfw IV Ausf D of Panzerregiment 25, part of Rommel's 7. Panzerdivision in France in 1940. While most of the crew wear the Panzer black double-breasted uniform with the early *Schutzmütze*, the commander, Oberst Karl Rothenburg, is wearing typical German Army uniform, with a ribbon bar that includes various World War I medals including the Blue Max. On his breast pocket he sports the NSDAP Golden Party badge. (NARA)

terms of training, organizing, and developing tactical and operational leadership. This was largely the product of the Reichswehr's personnel selection process.

It was not just the training that was good. The Germans realized that the key to armored success was leadership. The tank commanders had to be aggressive, bold but not foolhardy, and flexible. One German officer remembered: "The German superiority at this time lay not primarily in their equipment—the PzKpfw Is and IIs were not better than many French or Soviet models—but in their standards of training. The training of tank crews never ceased, even in combat. In 17. Panzerdivision, for example, it was the practice to hold a critique after each engagement, in which successes and failures were discussed, just as after peacetime exercises."

Before 1939, the tactical use of armored vehicles in combat had had a limited runout during the Spanish Civil War (1936–39). While the tactics had been examined carefully during and after this war, analysis of what had taken place in Spain led to very different interpretations. The Nazis provided the Nationalists with a little over one hundred PzKpfw I tanks under the command of Oberst Wilhelm von Thoma. In reality, the small scale of the number of tanks employed and the restrictions on their use didn't allow for any major conclusions. Von Thoma noted that Franco wanted to use the Panzers to support the infantry, rather than offensively in concentrations. Nevertheless:

> The combination of tanks with motorized infantry qualified armored units to accomplish many combat tasks in which both types of units complemented each other. … The speed of tanks on the march and in combat made command and timely appraisal of the situation very difficult. Close cooperation with aircraft was therefore necessary for command, reconnaissance, and combat.

The tank crews involved in Spain added to the professionalism of the German Army as it expanded rapidly after Hitler came to power. Elsewhere, in September 1937, the first large-scale tank training maneuvers were held around Neustrelitz.

With the approach of war, the programs for officer training were expanded and sped up. In 1940, U.S. observers estimated that schools were turning out about 6,500 officers every four months, and that 30,000 new officers entered the army between September 1939 and December 1940. The huge expansion of the German Army in the late 1930s—to six times its peacetime figure—brought obvious problems. Many reserve officers and NCOs had to be commissioned, as did veterans of World War I, and civilians were appointed to administrative posts (*Beamten*).

Great attention was also paid to "continuation" training of officers in the field.

Uniforms

This is a complicated subject, with significant differences in uniform (particularly pockets), piping, colors, and collar patches. While there were official introductions of new specifications—for example, the removal of

Black Panzer Model M43 visored field cap for enlisted men. (www.themarshalsbaton.com)

the skull from collar patches—there were time lags as to when these changes were actually rolled out on the battlefield. Additionally, many people involved in armored divisions who shouldn't have worn the black uniform did so. Even generals' collar insignia were seen on black tunics.

The black M1934 uniform, with its double-breasted jacket and Prussian hussar skulls, was distinctive. It identified not just Panzer crew, who were originally the only ones allowed to wear it, but most of the constituent elements of the *Panzertruppen*. Officially, the uniform comprised the M1934 jacket and pants, dark-gray shirt (no pockets, four buttons on front, until 1943; thereafter, two pleated breast pockets until replaced by gray-green shirt), gray sweatshirt, black tie, and black, laced boots (or in the case of the *Pioniere*, marching boots). It was introduced on November 12, 1934 and opened up to: *Nachrichten-Abteilungen* (signals) on April 2, 1937; *Artillerie-Regimenter* (artillery) in mid-1938; *Panzer-Aufklärungs-Abteilungen* (reconnaissance) in March 1940; and *Pioniere-Bataillone* (armored engineers) on May 10, 1940.

The jacket collar was piped—there were no NCOs' *Tresse*—there were shoulder boards, some of which had unit ciphers (A for Aufklärung; GD for Großdeutschland; L for Lehr; P for Panzerjäger). The *Spieß* kept his *Kolbenringe*. Pants were wool with a stirrup foot but were cut generously with either a built-in belt or belt loops.

Originally, Panzer crew wore the distinctive *Schutzmütze* two-part black beret—a rubber skullcap with a black wool outer. After March 27, 1940, this was replaced by the M1940 black *Feldmütze*. There were versions of this for officers and other ranks, although the *feldgrau* peaked caps were also used, as were *Schirmmütze*, particularly by tank commanders. In 1943 a black *Einheitsmütze* became available. The only problem was that its peak got in the way when using sights, so it wasn't particularly popular.

The black uniform details altered slightly. The M1936 had three small buttons and buttonholes added to the lapels and in 1942 the lapels were narrowed while the piping was discontinued.

It was difficult to weather the winter conditions in a tank. As well as the cold, frost and ice formed inside the tank and then melted and dripped as temperatures rose, leading to electrical problems. To begin with, greatcoats and locally supplied clothing kept the extreme cold at bay. From the winter of 1942/43, proper reversible parkas and overtrousers

Group photo of *Panzertruppen* who had fought in Karelia and two Finnish officers, October 15, 1941. (SA-Kuva)

were made available in white/gray; similar clothing in various camouflage schemes also became available during the war (in particular, those used by the Waffen-SS).

Many tank crew used one-piece coveralls or fatigues in off-white, khaki, reed-green, or black—and some of them were dyed black. These buttoned from the neck to the crotch. The 1942 reed-green tank fatigues were similar in cut to the black uniforms except that they had large pockets in the jacket (breast) and pants (thigh), and they also appeared in camo colors.

The biggest uniform difference between *Panzertruppen* and *Sturmgeschütz* crews (the latter being classified as artillery and wearing red piping) came with the introduction in May 1940 of the *feldgrau* version of the Panzer jacket and trousers. This *feldgrau* uniform was also used by *Pioniere* (1941 onwards), *Panzerjäger* and *SP Artillerie* (1942 onwards), *Aufklärungs* units (1943 onwards), and *Panzergrenadiere* (from 1944 onwards).

Luftwaffe tank units used the same uniform as the German Army but with different piping and, latterly, collar patches. Waffen-SS tank units used a similar tunic (although with a slightly different wrap-over cut and different collars) in black and *feldgrau*, and a black side cap was introduced in 1942.

Karl Roßmann commanded I. Abteilung of Panzerregiment Hermann Göring from July 1, 1942, first as a *Hauptmann* and then from January 1, 1944, as a *Major*. He surrendered to the Americans in 1945 as an *Oberstleutnant*. He's wearing the Luftwaffe version of the tanker's black uniform. Note his cuff title, the Luftwaffe insignia above the breast pocket, and the German Cross in Gold (awarded in June 1944) below it. (Wikipedia Commons)

Left: This young Panzer officer is wearing the German equivalent of the Sam Browne: the *Leibriemen mit Schulterriemen 34*—belt and cross strap—introduced in 1934. It had a two-spike silver buckle with a belt and cross strap. Its use was officially stopped in November 1939. Note the lack of the national emblem on the right breast, and the narrower collar, of this early Panzer jacket. (RCT)

Below left: Winter 1941 and this Panzer officer is disdaining gloves and warm footwear and wearing gaiters and ankle boots, an M34 jacket and field cap. Note the pink piping denoting armored corps around both collar and *Kragpatten* (collar patches). He has an EK II ribbon on his tunic and wears a Panzer Assault Badge. (Ian Spring/Pixpast.com)

Below and Right: Classic Wolfgang Willrich artwork showing a tank driver. Note the early headphones with orange ear protectors. Until 1941 only three of the tank crew— radioman, driver, and commander— were connected by intercom. In 1941 a new amplifying intercom box arrived, and the gunner joined the party. The loader was still out in the cold, but his duties required him to obtain ammunition from locations around the tank, so headset and microphone wires would be impractical. The new box meant new headphones, everyone receiving 2,000 ohm Dfh.b headsets with Kmfb throat mikes for commander and radioman. Illustrated (right) are Model "C" Bakelite microphones attached to leather-wrapped neckband with electrical connection cord and activation switch in housing. (RCT; www.themarshalsbaton.com)

Panzer officer's crusher *Schirmmütze* with *rosa* Panzer piping. (www.themarshalsbaton.com)

Waffenfarbe Piping

Antitank (*Panzerjäger*) in Pz or PzGren Div.	*Rosa* (pink)
Armor	*Rosa*, except Pz Reg 24 (24.PzDiv): *goldgelb* (golden yellow)
Armored reconnaissance (*Panzeraufklärung*)	*Goldgelb*—for most, except 1., 2., 4., 5. PzDivs: *rosa*; newly formed units *kupferbraun* (copper brown); from March 1943: *rosa* (official), *goldgelb* (often seen); from November 1944: *goldgelb* (official)
Artillery (*Artillerie*)	*Hochrot* (bright red)
Assault guns (*Sturmgeschütze*)	1939: *hochrot*; March 1943: *hochrot*, unless in infantry unit (white) or *Panzergrenadier* unit *wiesengrün* (meadow green)
Cavalry (*Kavallerie*)	*Goldgelb*
Chaplains (*Feldgeistliche*)	*Violett* (purple)
Construction (*Bautruppen*)	*Hellbraun* (light brown) until 1943, then *schwarz* (black)
Engineers (*Pioniere*)—combat armored, etc.	Alternating black/white on black uniform, black on *feldgrau* uniform
Generals (*Generalstabsoffiziere*)	*Karmesin* (carmine)
Infantry (*Infanterie*)	*Weiß* (white)
Light infantry (*Jäger*)	*Hellgrün* (light green, also *Jägergrün*)
Medics (*Sanitätstruppen*)	*Kornblumenblau* (cornflower blue)
Motorcycle infantry (*Kradschützen*)	*Kupferbraun*
Motorized reconnaissance (*Aufklärung*)	*Kupferbraun*
Mountain troops (*Gebirgsjäger*)	*Hellgrün*
MPs (*Feldgendarmerie*)	*Orange*
Nebelwerfer	*Bordeauxrot* (Bordeaux red)
Officials (*Beamte*)	*Dunkelgrün* (dark green)
Panzergrenadiere	*Wiesengrün*
Propaganda	*Lichtgrau* (light gray)
Recce in infantry & mountain div	1939: *goldgelb*; September 1943: *weiß*
Signals (*Nachrichten*)	*Hellbraun* until 1937; then *zitronengelb* (lemon yellow)
Ski troops (*Skijäger*)	*Hellgrün* (light green)
Supply troops (*Nachschubtruppen*)	*Blau* (blue)
Transport (*Kraftfahrtruppen*)	*Blau*

Above: Black panzer wrap for an Obergefreiter in the Grossdeutschland Panzerkorps. Shoulder straps are black backed with pink piping and embroidered with "GD." Note cuff title. (www.themarshalsbaton.com)

Above left: For all the heat of the desert, the tropical greatcoat was essential in North Africa—as shown by the crew of this PzKpfw IV Ausf D of Panzerregiment 8, 15. Panzerdivision. Note the divisional marking by the driver's slit. (Battlefield Historian)

Right: Gefreiter's 1940 first model tropical tunic in olive-green cotton twill. Note cuff title, *Totenköpfe* on lapels, and pink shoulderboard piping. (www.themarshalsbaton.com)

Below: In the desert, uniform—or lack of it—was less strictly controlled than elsewhere, as this photograph shows. Photographed by DAK commander Erwin Rommel himself on their PzKpfw III Ausf E, the uniforms worn by this tank crew have been faded by the sun to varying degrees. Note the faded tropical field caps, shirts, and shorts, the use of which was limited to keep sunburn to a minimum, and at left the long M1940 *Tropenstiefel*—tropical boots made of olive canvas and tan leather—that laced up to just below the knee. By the left-hand man's leg is a tropical helmet (*Tropenhelm*), showing the right-hand side with its black/white/red shield. The stubby barrel of the tank's 5 cm KwK L/42 main gun is adorned with an unusual "kill" marking—an RAF aircraft dated May 16, 1941. Alongside is the coaxial 7.92 cm MG34 machine gun and the open vision port for its operator who also loaded the main gun. (GF Collection)

Above: After the problems of the winter of 1941/42, by winter 1942 the German Army had got the right equipment to the front in time. A Leibstandarte column on the outskirts of Kharkov in March 1943. 555 is a PzKpfw III, while 559 and 558 in front are PzKpfw IIs. Note the white one-piece *Panzerkombi* suit worn by the man with binoculars on 555's turret. (GF Collection)

Below left: The M1942 padded reversible winter suit made a big difference—as, no doubt, did the flamboyant coat being worn by Count Hyazinth Strachwitz von Gross-Zauche und Camminetz (yes, that's all one name!). Strachwitz was wounded at Stalingrad with 16. Panzerdivision, was lucky enough to be evacuated, and when he recovered, took command of a tank regiment of the Heer's elite Großdeutschland Division. The PzKpfw IV Ausf G behind is camouflaged in a mix of lime and chalk—in the end, it depended on what was available. (GF Collection)

Below right: Well-wrapped 5. Panzerdivision PzKpfw III crewman taking a smoke break through the double-door escape hatch. The door on the right has a closed air/vision port, while the other has a glass vision block. By March 1942 the new Panzerkasten 20 meant that only the loader was omitted from the net. When there was a call for radio silence, the radio man simply switched off the radio receivers and switched to *Funk u. Bord* and only the internal intercom worked. (NAC)

Above left: Typical SS tank-crew black uniforms: note tank commander SS-Oberscharführer (T/Sgt) Horst Gresiak's "crusher" *Schirmmütze* and headphones, SS lapel rank insignia and upper-arm national eagle, and gunner's holstered sidearm. As an *Obersturmführer* (first lieutenant) Gresiak led 7. /SS-Panzer-Regiment 2 of 2. SS-Panzerdivision Das Reich. He's seen atop a PzKpfw III Ausf L; note on the turret side the lack of both gunner's vision port (deleted from the Ausf L) and *Nebelwurfgerät* (smoke discharger which was brought in from the Ausf M) and the AA MG34 mounting. (Akira Takiguchi Collection)

Above right: The tank commander was the boss, but the radio operator provided him with his links to the outside world. The tanks in a typical platoon were equipped with an FuG5 which paired a 10 W transmitter and an ultra-shortwave receiver with a transmitting range of 2.5 miles (4 km) using voice or 4.3 miles (7 km) in Morse code. This enabled them to speak to each other as well as internally within each tank. Platoon leaders had an extra ultra-shortwave receiver to talk to other platoons. Other setups allowed communication with the regimental command net, close air support aircraft, artillery, etc.[15] (NARA)

Inset, above left: Black wool field cap for a Waffen-SS Panzer officer. (www.themarshalsbaton.com)

Left: SS-Sturmbannführer Heinz von Westernhagen, commander of sSS-Pz Abt 101, runs a briefing near Beauvais in 1944. Assorted SS and Panzer uniforms include the M43 one-piece lightweight spring oak-leaf-pattern camouflage uniform, an Adolf Hitler cuff title (at third from right), and what looks like an Italian M41 field cap. (GF Collection)

Above left: Kurt Meyer in 1943. While commanding the Leibstandarte Aufklärungs-Abteilung during the battle of Kharkov, he and his men were responsible for massacring civilians, something that continued when he commanded the SS-Panzerdivision Hitlerjugend in Normandy. He's wearing a one-piece winter uniform. A convicted war criminal, his death sentence was commuted to life imprisonment though his extradition to the Soviet Union was refused. Meyer was able to leave jail early and live out his life (he died in 1961) promoting the idea of a "clean" Waffen-SS. (GF Collection)

Above right: Men of 5. SS-Panzerdivision's Panzerregiment 6 wearing spring oak-leaf-pattern camouflage coveralls. The Waffen-SS camouflaged tank wrap jackets and coveralls came in a number of forms: *Eichenlaub*—oak-leaf pattern or dapple camouflage—was used between 1941 and 1945; the stocks of Italian *Telo mimetico* that the Germans took over in 1943 were used until 1945; *Erbsenmuster*—also known as Pea pattern, Dot 44, or *Trompfenmuster*—was used 1944–45.[16] (NARA)

Below: SS-Panzerdivision Wiking O group (orders group) during *Unternehmen Ihlse* (around Kovel in Poland) during April/May 1944 as SS-Hauptsturmführer Alois Reicher (second from right), *Kommandeur* of II./SS-PzRegt 5, discusses the situation with the officers of Kampfgruppe Wühle. Reicher is wearing a Model 1937 SS officer's crusher cap and a greatcoat. At right, SS-Untersturmführer Alfred Großrock, who commanded 6./SS-PzRegt 5, is wearing a black SS Panzer uniform and a Waffen-SS officer's service cap with the silver bullion chin cords. The combination of the black uniform and skull is why Panzer crew, with their black M1934 uniform and skull collar patches, were mistaken for the SS. Note that the position of the SS *Hoheitsabzeichen*—the eagle that the Heer wore above the right breast pocket—is on the left upper arm above the Wiking cuff title. (NARA)

An officer from the *Aufklärungsabteilung* of 22. Panzerdivision in 1943—there's an SdKfz 232 eight-wheeled armoured car behind him. He's wearing his gray shirt collar outside his jacket and sports an EK II ribbon as well as two badges. The left-hand one is the *Deutsches Reichssportabzeichen in Silber* (German Reich Sports Badge in silver); on the right the *Panzerkampfabzeichen* (Panzer Assault Badge). (Ian Spring/Pixpast.com)

Below: The practical black Panzer uniform was introduced in 1934; it was a short and close-fitting jacket (M34) with no external pockets to snag, double-breasted for warmth, and black to hide lubricant stains, and the pants were cut generously wide. This *Panzermann* wears a collar and tie and the black *Feldmütze* (field cap) that replaced the *Schutzmütze* in winter 1939/40. He's photographed in Germany in 1941, just before his unit—Panzerregiment 33 of 9. Panzerdivision—went to Romania. (Ian Spring/Pixpast.com)

Soldier from 22. Panzerdivision beside the River Sèvre Niortaise in Niort where the division was formed in late September 1941. After training in Brittany, the division moved to the Soviet Union in March 1942. He's wearing the typical Panzer uniform. (Ian Spring/Pixpast.com)

Awards and Decorations

Panzer crew can be seen wearing much the same decorations and badges as the rest of the Wehrmacht. From the awards for bravery, such as the Iron Cross, to the more common wound badges, *Panzertruppen* received the same general awards. (These are covered in a companion volume on the German infantryman.) However, as with the other arms of service, there were several awards that were specialized, the most obvious of which was the *Panzerkampfabzeichen*.

In 1921, the *Erinnerungsabzeichen für ehemalige Besatzungen deutscher Kampfwagen* (Commemorative badge for former crew members of German tanks) was instituted for those who had fought in tanks in World War I. The Spanish Civil War saw the *Panzertruppenabzeichen der Legion Condor* awarded to tank crew who had served in theater for three months or more. In 1939 at the behest of the German Army's Commander-in-Chief, Generaloberst Walther von Brauchitsch, the *Panzerkampfwagenabzeichen* (Tank Badge) was authorized. Redesigned by the Berlin firm of Wilhelm Ernst Peekhaus, the silver badge was first introduced in December 1939 and was awarded to tank crew who had (a) participated in three armored assaults over three separate days; (b) been wounded in an assault; or (c) had earned a bravery award during an assault. Subsequently, on June 6, 1940, a bronze version was instituted to be awarded to other units serving in armored vehicles with Panzer divisions—Panzergrenadiers, for example.

In June 1943, four new classes were instituted in both silver and bronze to reward participation in 25, 50, 75, and 100 armored actions.

Below, Left to Right: *Allgemeines Sturmabzeichen* (General assault badge) awarded to participants in an infantry attack who weren't infantry e.g., engineers, Sturmgeschütz crew, tank crew fighting as infantry); *Panzerkampfabzeichen*; *Panzerkampfabzeichen* for 75 armored actions. (Big Fish121 at the English Wikipedia [CC BY-SA 3.0 DEED]; GF Collection; Gary Todd, Wiki Commons [CC0 1.0])

These *Aufklärungsabteilung* officers have been attending a strategy conference in Rostov in July 1942—a lecture is taking place behind them. Note the yellow *Waffenfarbe*, indicating reconnaissance (this changed to pink in 1943), the black two-pronged leather belts worn by officers (as compared to the belt buckle on ORs' belts, see p. 36) and the medals and badges. Left-hand *Leutnant* (shoulder-strap unit identifier indistinguishable) looks like he has a Sports badge; right-hand *Leutnant* has a ribbon bar with EK II and Sudetenland Medal ribbons. Below he has an EK I on his breast pocket, with a wound badge and the bronze *Panzerkampfabzeichen* awarded to recon troops, *Panzergrenediere* etc. Note the flap and button on pants' pockets. (Ian Spring/Pixpast.com)

Other awards, such as the *Allgemeines Sturmabzeichen* (General Assault Badge) instituted originally for combat engineers in 1940 and the *Sonderabzeichen für das Niederkämpfen von Panzerkampfwagen durch Einzelkämpfer* (Tank Destruction Badge), were also worn by tank crew who had fought as infantry or by other soldiers from Panzer divisions.

On October 17, 1938, a new *Schützenschnur*, or Marksmanship/gunnery proficiency lanyard, was instituted for armored troops' NCOs and men—officers didn't wear them. They came in several levels: 1–4 had a tank in a ring; 5–8 had a tank in oak-leaf wreath; and 9–12 had the same in gold. Shortly after, the regular acorns that hung from it were changed to gun shells.

Right: A *Panzermann* on leave playing with his son (note the latter's *Kolbenringe*—the piston rings of a *Spieß*!). The soldier is wearing a Panzer *Schützenschnur*. (RCT)

Below right: An Iron Cross award ceremony for tank drivers of 22. Panzerdivision in Kherson 1942. Medals are important to soldiers—and while many were awarded (as many as 4.5 million EK IIs in the war), they still meant something. Friedrich Sander says, tongue in cheek, in his diary on receiving his, "now I have visible proof that I am not a coward." He also alludes to the informality of these award ceremonies in the field. (Ian Spring/Pixpast.com)

Left: Oberst Richard Koll was CO of Panzerregiment 11 in 6. Panzerdivision, and he fought in France and during *Barbarossa*. He ended the war as a *Generalleutnant*, chief of Wehrmacht Motor Transport. He wears the silver *Panzerkampfabzeichen*, a silver DRL sports badge and a wound badge, as well as the *Spange zum Eisernen Kreuz* (Clasp to the Iron Cross) worn over the top of a 1914 Iron Cross. (Bundesarchiv Bild 101I-208-0030-05)

| The Units

The *Balkenkreuz*, harking back to the symbol of the Teutonic Knights, was used as the national identifier—of particular importance on the many *Beutepanzer*. At the start of the war, this was a solid white cross on the front and sides of tanks; after the fighting in Poland, the solid cross was made hollow with a white outline; in 1943, as *dunkelgelb* became the primary color for Panzers, a black cross with a white outline was introduced. In August 1944 this changed again, with the white outline being altered to red, with the cross only appearing on tanks, armored cars, and assault guns. However, this modification doesn't seem to have appeared in practice to any great degree.

Aerial identification was important to reduce blue-on-blue attacks. A great variety of symbols and media was used for this, including *Balkenkreuz* and *Hakenkreuz* (swastika) flags (black swastika in a solid white circle on a red background, etc.).

Panzer Organization, Unit Numbering, and Markings

The Wehrmacht used a mixture of Arabic and Roman numerals and names to identify its units. Thus:

- *Heeresgruppe (army group) Nord/Mitte/Süd (North/Center/South)*
- *6. Armee (army; pl. Armeen) also 2. Panzerarmee*
- *XL. Armeekorps (pl. the same)*
- *Panzergruppe 2 or Guderian (pl. -en)*
- *6. Panzerdivision (pl. -en)*
- *Panzerbrigade 3 (pl. -n)*
- *Panzerregiment 2 (pl. -er)*
- *Panzerabteilung Rhodos (Pz Bn Rhodes) or PzAbt 216 (pl. -en)*

Divisions were numbered using Arabic numerals (12. Panzerdivision), but their tactical signage used symbols or images rather than numbers. The divisions were divided into tank regiments (Panzerregiment 5) which were split into two or three regimental *Abteilungen* (battalions) numbered with Roman numerals (I./PzRegt 5).

Other *Abteilungen*, such as the heavy tank battalions, used Arabic numbers (sSS-PzAbt 101 = schwere SS-Panzerabteilung 101 = SS Heavy Tank Battalion 101; Aufklärungs-Abteilung 580 (mot.) in North Africa = Motorized Reconnaissance Battalion 580; Panzerabteilung 40 (Tank Battalion 40, which fought in Norway), or Panzerjäger Abteilung 654 (Tank Destroyer Battalion 654).

The regimental *Abteilungen* were divided into companies (*Kompanie/Kompanien*) with 1.–4. in I. Abteilung and 5.–8. in II. Abteilung. Each *Kompanie* was further divided into four platoons (*Zug/Züge*), each with an HQ and—where possible—four vehicles. These were numbered on the turret sides, usually with three black or red numbers with white outlines,

The grimy driver of a PzKpfw 38(t), a corporal, rests on the road to the Channel, May 1940. He's wearing a padded beret (as is the tank commander), an M1934 tank uniform, and goggles. They've both got a "Let's get this done" look. Note the new form of black-core *Balkenkreuz* identification. (Bundesarchiv_Bild_101I-769-0229-26)

Another early war photo showing a column that includes a Panzer II Ausf D and Panzer I Ausf B (nearest the camera). Note the *Schutzmützen* and black Panzer uniforms. There's a tactical rhomboid marking on the back of the turrets but no crosses. (GF Collection)

PzKpfw Is and IIs next to a SdKfz 251/3 Ausf A *mit Rahmenantenne*—a command vehicle with a frame aerial. The column of vehicles has halted at the Brda River in Poland on September 3, 1939, and it's possible General Heinz Guderian, commander of XIX Armeekorps, is in the command SPW. Note the plain-white *Balkenkreuz* on the vehicles. It was used until early 1940 and was replaced by the black-core cross. (Bundesarchiv, Bild 146-1976-071-36 / CC-BY-SA 3.0)

A *Signal* magazine image showing PzKpfw IV Ausf E 414 in Ukraine, 1942. Note the "K" for Kleist, the *dunkelgrau* paint scheme, and the *Balkenkreuz* formed from white-only paint application. (GF Collection)

but the colors depended on the background. They needed to be visible enough to allow command and control, but not so visible that they would stand out as aiming marks for antitank gunners.

The system of numbering wasn't straightforward. The standard rule was that the first number signified the company, the second the platoon, and the third the position in the platoon, with HQ and staff vehicles having other identifying features. Thus, 821 meant 8. Kompanie, 2. Zug, 1st tank in troop = commander's vehicle. If the second number was an "0," it was a company HQ vehicle. Sometimes the first number was replaced by an "R" for a regimental staff tank; battalion vehicles might use Roman "I" or "II" first for command vehicles. The first Tigers in Panzerregiment Großdeutschland were number S01 (Stabs-Zug) S10–S13 (1. Zug) and S20–23 (2. Zug). However, this system became too obvious for continued use in the field, as the enemy got wise to it and tried to knock out command vehicles first. To get around this, units often used different systems, including four-digit numbers.

These tactical numbers were originally painted in white onto rhomboid metal plates; later they were hand-painted onto turret sides. For unturreted assault guns and Panzerjäger, they were usually placed above the *Balkenkreuz* (bar cross).

PzKpfw IV Ausf D in 1941. Note that the commander is wearing a black jacket while his crew are in shirtsleeve order, the equipment box at rear of turret (first seen on the Ausf D), and the single-door hatch—double doors came in on the F1. It's numbered 821, 8 = company, 2 = platoon, 1 = position in platoon. (Leo Marriott collection)

There were many other tactical symbols and letters used—from the "K" and "G" identifying Panzergruppen Kleist and Guderian in the invasion of France, to the more complicated use of German standard tactical symbols for "B" vehicles.

Establishments

The German equivalent of U.S. T/O&E (tables of organization and equipment) or British war establishment were the *Gliederung* (formations), *Kreigsstärkenachweisung* (KStN—lit. proof of war strength) allied to the *Kriegsausrüstungsnachweis* (KAN—table of equipment). The first identified the organization, the second the manpower, and the third their equipment.

There are hundreds of these tables, and when you include those modified by Army Orders (*Heeresmittelungen*) and different theaters, there are just too many to reproduce sensibly. Added to this, Panzers appeared in many different types of unit, each with a different organization and complement of vehicles.

On paper, the German Panzer division of 1939 had 11,790 men and 328 tanks. These were divided into two brigades (Panzer and infantry) of two regiments, each with four battalions (one of the infantry regiments was motorized). There were supporting units

Right: Tactical signage was used throughout a division's assets. This towed 2 cm Flak 30 shows the 1. Panzerdivision marking. (GF Collection)

Below: PzKpfw IV Ausf J with its long 7.5 cm KwK 40 L/48 in Nyíregyháza, north of Debrecen late 1944. Note the opened and folded turret standoff armor that allowed access to the turret double hatch. The five crewmen seem to be drinking from both a bottle and a large jar of liquid. Driver, radio operator, and loader (on far side) all wear the black peaked *Einheitsmütze*; the commander and gunner have *Feldmützen*. The commander and gunner appear to carry shields on their left arms: the size and shape indicates possibly *Krimschild* (Crimean campaign of 1941/42) or *Kubanschild* (Kuban bridgehead of 1943) but they are too indistinct to be sure. Note, too, the outline turret number 332 and the blocked-in *Balkenkreuz* over the later war camouflage. (NAC)

(e.g., *Aufklärungs*, *Pioniere*, *Nachrichten*, and *Artillerie*). However, rarely did a division (or any unit, come to that) have exactly what it should have had on paper, and even if it did, any unit with tanks would usually have some of them undergoing repair (especially if they were in combat). It was just the same for men: leave, sickness, training, death—there were any number of reasons why the number of troops would differ from the paper strength.

The German way of reporting these numbers adds to the general confusion. Up to 1942, units had to supply this information three times a month:[17]

- *Sollstärke* = authorized strength (linked into the KStN)
- *Iststärke* = actual strength
- *Fehlstellen* = the difference between the two
- *Gefechtstärke* = battle strength (not to include staff, medics, stretcher bearers, baggage trains)
- *Verpflegungsstärke* = ration strength (men and horses; including those on leave and those the unit was responsible for supporting—e.g., crews in repair depots waiting for their vehicles; HiWis; PoWs, etc.)

This changed in late 1942 so that only information pertaining to *Gefechtstärke*, *Verpflegungsstärke*, *Iststärke*, and altering the exclusions (e.g., removing temporarily assigned units and personnel on leave or duties with another unit from the *Verpflegungsstärke*) had to be supplied.

There was another change in April 1944. By then, the organization of German divisions had changed significantly. The Panzer division's KStN now included 14,750 men but only about 160 tanks. There was one armored regiment with two tank battalions (one equipped with Panthers, the other PzKpfw IVs) and two infantry regiments, each with two battalions, along with supporting units, including an artillery regiment of three batteries (one tracked and two motorized—one light, one heavy). Including the various staff vehicles, this gave a paper strength of 78 PzKpfw IV, 73 Panther, three PzBefWg IV, six PzBefWg Panther,

Propaganda footage being shot by a *Kriegsberichter* (war correspondent) embedded with 3. Panzerdivision. Note the tactical signs showing: at left, the Berlin bear in black-on-yellow (the division was formed at Wünsdorf about 12.4 miles [20 km] south of Berlin) which was introduced in September 1941, and, at right, the tactical symbol for the 3. Division as used in the second half of 1942. Only 58 of the Daimler-Benz SdKfz 247 Ausf B (the *schwerer geländegängiger gepanzerter Personenkraftwagen*, to give it its full name) were produced for use by commanders of motorcycle and reconnaissance battalions. Retrofitted with radios, they could carry driver, co-driver, and four other people depending on radio load. (GF Collection)

White on dark background (probably green) Afrika Korps symbol on 823 of 8./Panzerregiment 5, one of a number of vehicles that carried this number in North Africa. (GF Collection)

two Bergepanzer III, and eight Flakpanzer IV—along with 21 Jagdpanzer IV, 6 Hummel, 12 Wespe, 6 ammo carriers, and 5 *Artillerie-Beobachtungswagen* (observation vehicles). The equivalent Waffen-SS Panzer divisions were even bigger, often much closer to the paper strength. They had six battalions of infantry, and some had a paper strength of as many as 20,000 men.

The reality, of course, was very different. Tanks are sensitive instruments and there's a lot to go wrong with them—and that's before people try to shoot at them, drop bombs on them, or lay mines. The units had to supply similar reports on the tank strengths—whether they were operational, in repair, or write-offs. In some cases, at some specific moments divisions might not have any tanks which were operational. Take as an (extreme) example the Panthers in *Unternehmen Zitadelle*, their first action. When this action started on July 5, 1943, 184 Panthers entered the arena (already 16 shy of the 200 delivered); by July 7 only 40 were operational. By July 10 that figure was down to 10. It rose to 44 on July 17. On July 20 the status of their Panthers was: operational 41, repairable in theater 85, repairable in Germany 16, and total write-offs 58.

This excellent photograph is full of detail. It was taken as German 12. Armee advanced from Bulgaria into Yugoslavia and shows a PzKpfw IV Ausf E of 11. Panzerdivision whose *Gespenster* (ghost) symbol is apparent next to the open-work *Balkenkreuz* and below the two-digit turret tank number. There's an additional 11.PD marking—a broken circle and bar—on this and the tank behind. The under-barrel frame was to push aside the aerial when traversing. The big change with the Ausf E was the realization that the armor needed to be increased, and the appliqué armor bolted on to the upper front and side plates is apparent. Note too, the tool stowage and the mounting step in the "Up" position below the gunner's hand. The variation of official and casual dress is interesting. The commander wears the Panzer uniform, the gunner a lightweight jacket and an M38 side cap without piping, and the driver wears a V-neck sweatshirt and M38 side cap with piping. (Bundesarchiv, Bild 101I-770-0280-20/Feitel, Dr./[CC-BY-SA 3.0])

Panzer Divisions

The main building block of most army units in World War II was the division—the smallest unit that could act independently. The first three Panzer divisions were raised in 1935, and by the start of World War II there were five Panzer divisions and five *leichte Divisionen*—light divisions that had an *Abteilung* of 88 tanks, but which were basically organized as motorized infantry divisions. These were later converted to Panzer divisions. The Panzer divisions were at the forefront of most German undertakings and suffered accordingly. Many of them were destroyed and reconstituted—some, such as those at Stalingrad or in Tunisia, were reconstituted after capture.

The constituent elements of the Panzer divisions changed regularly, but all had a HQ and HQ unit, administrative, MP (*Feldgendarmerie*), supply (*Nachschub*), medical (*Sanitäts*), and field post office (*Feldpostamt*) elements. The key fighting units were the Panzer and Panzergrenadier regiments. Before 1942, the Panzer division's infantry were called *Schützen* (riflemen); they became "*Panzergrenadiere*" when Hitler decided that infantrymen would become *Grenadiere* in 1942. Typical of the complications of German Army insignia, the *Schützen* had worn pink *Waffenfarbe* and the motorized infantry white, and when they became *Panzergrenadiere* they all changed to *Wiesengrün* (meadow green) … except, of course, some didn't, instead wearing the Panzer pink till the end.

Panzer divisions had their complement of *Aufklärungs* (reconnaissance) troops, at first using motorcycles (*Kradschützen*—motorcycle troops), although these proved less than efficient in North Africa and the Soviet Union: armored cars (wheeled and half-tracked, usually variants of the SdKfz 250), Kübelwagen/Schwimmwagen, or other vehicles took their place.

Panzer artillery and *Panzerjäger* units got heavier as the war progressed: the first divisions had towed artillery; later in the war, SP guns—such as the 10.5 cm armed Wespe and the later, heavier Hummel with a 15 cm gun—proliferated. The first *Panzerjäger* were the Marder series using captured guns on obsolescent—Pzkpfw I or 38(t)—or French chassis. These also got heavier as the war progressed with the Nashorn and Elefant/Ferdinand. The elephant in the room here is the Sturmgeschütz III/IV that ended up being the German jack-of-all-trades AFV, combining infantry support with longer-gunned, tank-killing roles. It and its crews came under the artillery rather than Panzer arm and will be dealt with in a separate book.

The first Panzer divisions had light 2 cm antiaircraft guns, but as the war progressed antiair became more and more important. Initially towed, these guns were mounted on halftracks and after 1943 Flakpanzers—AA guns mounted on various Panzer chassis—came in. From 1944, a Flak section was included in a Panzer division's establishment.

The key additional units in the Panzer division were the *Nachrichten* (signals), *Pioniere* (engineers), and, of course, the maintenance unit.

As well as divisions, many independent *Abteilungen* were formed usually because of special circumstances, such as the Panther *Abteilungen* (51 and 52) used at Kursk.

This April 1941 photograph shows Panzerregiment 36 of 14. Panzerdivision in Zagreb. The men are readying their vehicles for return to Germany from whence the regiment was transported east by rail for *Unternehmen Barbarossa*. This photograph is from the negatives left behind by Josef Kleffner, who was killed in action at Stalingrad. (*Akira Takiguchi Collection*)

Schwere Panzerabteilungen (Heavy Tank Battalions)

A number of units—such as those employing heavy tanks, heavy *Panzerjäger*, *Sturmpanzer*, *Sturm-Mörser*, and *Funklenk* radio-controlled tanks—weren't parceled out to divisions but kept in their own *Abteilungen* and attached to units as required. The Tigers were undoubtedly the most effective heavy tank of the war. In action from 1942, they performed heroically in defense—not the mission they were built for—and usually had high kill-to-loss ratios in their favor. They could take heavy punishment and proved very survivable. Most knocked-out Tigers were salvageable, with crews surviving the ordeal and returning to combat. This longevity added to the experience of the crews, as Wilbeck suggests,[18] and made them even deadlier opponents.

However, the Tigers also had major defects that reduced their efficiency:

- Tigers were too heavy for most recovery vehicles, and there were insufficient Bergepanthers (the best recovery vehicle for the job). This meant that many damaged or broken-down Tigers that could have been salvaged had to be destroyed by their crews. The weight also made bridging difficult and, especially in the retreat, hard to ferry across rivers. In total, some 40 percent of all Tiger losses are put down to

PzKpfw III of Pz-Regt 5, 2. Panzerdivision, during *Unternehmen Marita*. The division attacked towards Strumica in Yugoslavia before heading south into Greece and taking Thessaloniki. Note the tank's individual number (later in the war carried in larger letters on the turret sides) on metal plates at the rear and on the sides. The 201 indicates that this tank is 2. Kompanie's command element. Note also the rhomboid symbol with a 2, further indicating its role as a command vehicle. (NAC)

"destruction by crew," and many of these would have been the result of automotive or mechanical failure.

- They needed frequent maintenance and proved unreliable to the extent that it was rare for units to be able to field anywhere near their full quota of machines. This may have contributed to the longevity of their crews, but it meant that they were often only available in very small numbers.

- Their range was extremely small: Tiger I: 121 miles/195 km on 143 gal/540 l of fuel; Tiger II: 44 miles/170 km on 227 gal/860 l. Cross-country, in terms of speed, they'd be lucky to reach 12.5 mph/20 kph.

Below left: 8./SS-PzRegt 2 The tactical signage is more detailed on this vehicle. Sited on the front of a 21. Panzerdivision SdKfz 253 *leichter Gepanzerter Beobachtungskraftwagen* (light, amored observation vehicle), an enclosed version of the 250/1 that was used by artillery FOOs (this one has a frame aerial), the split-D divisional marking looks like a "B." Below is the symbol for a motorized artillery unit, the 3 indicating the 3. (mot.) Abteilung of 155. Panzer-Artillerie-Regiment which had a battery of 10 cm K18 heavy guns. (GF Collection)

Below right: PzKpfw III Ausf J command vehicle of SS-Panzerabteilung 5 from SS-Division (mot.) Wiking, as the divisional symbol on front track guard shows. The Ausf J had various improvements from previous models, including uparmoring—20 mm spaced armor was added to the gun mantlet from April 1942—a *Kugelblende* 50 ball-mounted hull machine gun, and an improved driver's visor. 1,000 of the c. 2,500 Ausf Js which were produced boasted the longer KwK 39 L/60 (as here). This photograph was taken in summer 1942 during the German offensive into the Caucasus. The camouflage scheme is *gelbbraun* (RAL 8000) as a base coat with *graugrün* (RAL 7008) as the secondary. Infantry ride on the back. On November 9, 1942, the division became the SS-Panzergrenadier Division Wiking. (NARA)

- There were painfully few of them. Expensive to produce at over RM250,000 (about $2 million today)—four times as much as a StuG III—only 1,347 Tiger Is had been built when production ceased in August 1944. The Tiger II was even more expensive at c. RM320,000 (about $2.5 million today), and only 492 had been completed by the end of the war.

Nevertheless, what is incontrovertible is the Tigers were good at what they were asked to do: kill other tanks. For the total loss of around 1,500 of their own—just under half of which were lost in action—they were responsible for the loss of significantly more of the enemy, with a ratio of 4:1 or 5:1 being likely.

The Tigers were organized into *Abteilungen*, initially companies of three platoons, each platoon having three tanks. This was the setup for the first three units, the regular army sPzAbt 501, 502, and 503 created in May 1942. Subsequently, in August 1942 the KStN changed to include 10 PzKpfw IIIs: a company HQ of a Tiger and two PzKpfw IIIs, and four platoons each of two Tigers and two PzKpfw IIIs. The actual organization in the field was more malleable but this KStN (1167d) was used for the first five *Abteilungen* (501–505) until May 1943:

- Bn HQ, two Tigers;

- three companies (although the third was rarely fielded because of lack of vehicles) of four platoons;

- HQ and supply company to include a light platoon of five PzKpfw IIIs; signals, AA, engineers, motorcycles, transport platoons, and a medical section;

- workshop company including a recovery platoon.

In March 1943 a new organization, KStN 1176e, led to changes, the main change being the loss of the PzKpfw IIIs. The new Abteilung was allocated 45 Tigers organized as:

- Bn HQ, three Tigers;

A Tiger of 8./SS-Pz-Regiment 2 Das Reich, this one showing the more usual symbol for the division, the *Wolfsangel* or wolf's hook. Here maintenance is taking place: note the removal of the exhaust stacks. (GF Collection)

- three companies (although the third was sometimes not fielded because of lack of vehicles) of HQ (two Tigers) and three platoons (each four Tigers);

- supply company to include signals, scout, AA, engineers, armored reconnaissance, and transport platoons, and a medical section;

- workshop company including a recovery platoon, two tracked and one wheeled maintenance platoons.

As well as the 10 *sPz-Abteilungen*, in spring 1943 a battalion was created for the Großdeutschland Panzergrenadier Division, and three *sSS-Pz-Abteilungen* (101, 102, and 103) were created, although sSS-PzAbt 103 didn't have vehicles until January 1944, and didn't reach full strength until January 1945. The *sSS-Pz-Abteilungen* changed their designations to 501, 502, and 503 leading to confusion and redesignation of the army units.

From November 1943, these *Abteilungen* began to receive Tiger IIs. By the end, 10 of the *Abteilungen* had received some Tiger IIs, but only six received the full complement of 45.

Three SS heavy tank companies were created in 1942–43: 13. Kompanie/1. SS-Panzerregiment Leibstandarte SS Adolf Hitler, 8. Kompanie/2. SS-Panzerregiment Das Reich, and 9. Kompanie/3. SS-Panzerregiment Totenkopf.

13./1. SS-PzRegt LSSAH fought from late 1943 till March 1944 at Kursk, in Italy, and at the Cherkassy pocket, before deactivation on March 1, 1944.

8./2. SS-PzRegt Das Reich was formed in December 1942, fought at Kharkov, Kursk, and as a *Kampfgruppe*, until March 27, 1944.

9./3. SS-PzRegt Totenkopf was set up in January 1943 and fought at Pavlograd, Kharkov, Kursk, Kharkov again, and Novo Alexandrovka. In April 1944 they fought in Romania before moving by train to take part in suppressing the Warsaw Uprising. Moving to Hungary, they took part in the three *Unternehmen Konrad* and *Frühlingerwachsen*. They retreated to Austria and surrendered to American forces who handed them over to the Soviets.

8./SS-Pz-Regiment 2 Das Reich was one of three heavy tank companies created in 1942–43 for SS divisions. It is said that its symbol of the *Springender Teufel* (jumping devil) was created after a figure found in Kharkov.[19] (NARA)

The Panzers

The first Panzers were very different to those used at the end of the war. Changes to vehicle size and complexity, to automotive systems and running gear, to tank weaponry and ammunition—the constant improvements to enemy vehicles and weapons meant that the Panzers had to develop— and the crewmen were continuously having to learn different ways of handling new equipment in battle. This is a brief survey of the main types of tank used by the Panzerwaffe.

Panzer I (SdKfz 101) and Kleiner Panzerbefehlswagen (SdKfz 265)

Crew: PzKpfw I had a two-man crew of commander and driver.

PzBefWg—had a three-man crew of commander, radio operator, and driver.

The development of tank design between 1932 and 1945 is well shown by comparing this, the first of the *Panzerkampfwagen*, with the behemoths of the final years of the war. The first of the Panzers were thinly armored and poorly armed with a pair of machine guns. The PzKpfw I weighed a mere 5.4 tons, measured 4.02 × 2.6 × 1.72 m (13.2 × 6.8 × 5.6 ft), and was crewed by a driver in the main body who used levers controlling the tracks to steer the tank, and a commander in the turret who also had to fire the guns. Communicating by a voice tube, the crew's main mission was against infantry and, before heavier antitank weapons were available, the PzKpfw I proved a useful battlefield tool that was improved upon from the Ausf A by the Ausf B's better engine and gearbox.

Most of the tanks that went to help Franco in the Spanish Civil War were PzKpfw I Ausf As, as here on the outskirts of Madrid. It's worth comparing this, the first German tank, with the last into full production: the Tiger II. The PzKpfw I weighed just over 5 tons and was 13 ft/4 m long. The Königstiger was 68 tons and 33.8 ft/10.3 m long. The speed of development was dictated by what happened on the battlefield, as each side alternately took the lead in an increasingly competitive arms race. (NAC)

The PzKpfw I Ausf B continued in service into 1943 as a command vehicle. Its size is well illustrated in this 1942 photograph of SS troops training in Karelia, Finland. (Image by Military Museum on the Finna service hosted by the Finnish Ministry of Education and Culture)

The PzKpfw I was used heavily in Nazi propaganda and was produced in sufficient numbers (including training tanks and command vehicles, over 2,000 were produced) to see prolific service from the Spanish Civil War (Spanish crews dubbed them *negrillo*, meaning little blackie), through the annexation of the Sudetenland and the attack in the West, to substantial use in *Barbarossa*. It went on to be converted for use as a *Panzerjäger* (armed with a Czech 4.7 cm PaK) and heavy infantry gun (armed with a sIG33 15 cm), as well as an ammunition carrier (SdKfz 111). Small numbers of other versions were produced.

Perhaps its most effective use, however, was as a training vehicle—with and without its superstructure. In many ways, the PzKpfw I was the most influential armored vehicle of the interwar period. It was the tank that trained the Panzerwaffe of the Blitzkrieg years, And it was also influential in gearing up German industry to tank production along with all that went with it—from optics to ammunition stowage, spare parts availability, and maintenance.

It also played a significant role being used as the first of the armored command vehicles. The Germans realized very quickly that command and control of their tanks was vital to the success of their battlefield tactics, and so all tanks were built with radio receivers.

The PzKpfw I Ausf A was underpowered and its engine overheated. Solving the problem led to the Ausf B, an increase in length, and an extra roadwheel. The Ausf A went to war with a with a plain-white Balkenkreuz and was armed with two 7.92 MG 13s. (Pollyanna1919/WikiCommons [CC BY-SA 3.0])

Additionally, they built around 200 PzKpfw Is without turrets and added a superstructure that allowed the inclusion of an FuG6 radio transmitter, the generator to power it, and a radio operator. Armament was limited to a single ball-mounted machine gun. After experience of combat in Poland, the *kleiner Panzerbefehlswagen* (as distinct from the *grosse*, the PzKpfw III version) was uparmored and the commander's vision under fire improved with a cupola. Larger frame aerials were also used, although they had the disadvantage of advertising the command role and attracting fire. The *kleiner Panzerbefehlswagen* made a valuable contribution to the control of Panzer units well into 1942.

Panzer II (SdKfz 121)

Crew: All Ausf except Ausf L had a three-man crew of commander/gunner, loader/radio operator, and driver.

Ausf L—four-man crew of commander (gunner), driver, loader, and radio operator.

The other early Panzer of the interwar years, the PzKpfw II, was quickly developed when it was realized that production of the PzKpfw III and IV was delayed. Early limited production versions (produced May 1936–July 1937) saw design improvements, and the Ausf A entered production by July 1937. Again, experience in Poland—over 80 PzKpfw IIs were destroyed, many by the Polish 7.9 mm Karabin przeciwpancerny wz.35 antitank rifle—quickly led to uparmoring, and from October 1940 a kit was introduced to improve the commander's vision with eight periscopes added to the cupola.

The PzKpfw II had a crew of three, with the driver to the left of the front hull withthe gearbox on his right. The loader/radio operator sat behind the driver with an FuG5 receiver and 10-watt transmitter—better radio communications than any other tank of the time, although there were engine interference problems that were difficult to resolve. The commander had a seat in the turret, from where he sighted and fired the 2 cm KwK 30 L/55 autocannon (later versions had the KwK 38 L/55) and 7.92 mm coaxial MG 34 machine gun). The autocannon used 10-round clips and fired at a nominal rate of 600 rounds/min, with an ammunition storage capacity of 180 shells.

Most Flammpanzer IIs were built from new, but 43 were converted from PzKpfw II Ds and Es. They were issued to two *Abteilungen* for Barbarossa, F100 and 101, which were attached to 18. and 7. Panzerdivisionen respectively. Late in 1941 many of the chassis were converted to become Marder Panzerjäger. The two flame nozzles at the front are covered; note also smoke dischargers at the rear. (NAC)

Above left: The PzKpfw II Ausf F was the final model and was armed with a 2 cm KwK 30 autocannon fed by a detachable box magazine. The skier has reversible armbands, red and black, to identify friend from foe, as both sides wore winter coveralls. (NAC)

Above right: This PzKpfw II Ausf A, seen during the Polish campaign, affords a close-up view of the NKAV smoke dispenser that was manufactured for use on German tanks until 1942. The dispenser was activated by the commander who pulled a control wire to drop the *Schnellnebelkerze* 39 smoke grenades behind the tank. They would give off smoke for two to three minutes, allowing the vehicle to reverse and escape. It wasn't very effective and was replaced by the turret-mounted *Nebelwurfgerät* (see p. 73). (Akira Takiguchi Collection)

There were various other improvements to the PzKpfw II, the uparmored Ausf F being the main one. There were variants, too. The Ausf L (SdKfz 123) Luchs was a redesign to produce a reconnaissance tank: 100 were built before production was stopped, and this meant an upgunned—from 2 cm to 5 cm—version was built. The Luchs had a crew of four: the driver and radio operator sat in the hull, and the commander (who was also the gunner) and loader sat in the turret. It used torsion bar suspension and *Schachtellaufwerk* overlapping roadwheels. Other PzKpfw II variants included *Brückenleger* (bridgelayer), *Flammpanzer* (tank armed with a flamethrower), Panzerjäger Marder II, using either the Soviet 76 mm (SdKfz 132) or German PaK 40 (SdKfz 131) gun, infantry support gun mounting a sIG33, and Wespe SP gun (SdKfz 124) mounting a 10.5 cm leFH18M. Nearly 700 of the Wespe were built.

Panzer 38(t)

Crew: All Ausf had a four-man crew of commander, gunner, loader, driver.

After the annexation of Czechoslovakia, the German Army tested the TNHP-S built by Cesko-moravska Kolben Denek of Prague—soon to be renamed Böhmisch-Mährische Maschinenfabrik AG. It was one of the best tanks available at the time, a marked improvement on the PzKpfw I and II. It would see service in various forms for the rest of the war. The numbers built were: Ausf A (150), B (110), C (110), D (105), E (275), F (250), S (321)—the first 90 of which were destined for Sweden but commandeered by the German Army—and G (90).

The Germans made two immediate and significant changes. The Czech Army had a three-man crew: the driver front right, the radio operator/bow gunner front left, and the commander (who also had to be gunner and loader) in the turret. The Germans immediately took out ammunition bins, reducing the rounds carried by 18, to include an extra crewman—a loader who would go to the left of the gun—although it must have been extremely cramped. The commander still had to fire the main gun, but at least he didn't have to load it as well. The main gun was the 3.7 cm A7 L/48.7 made by Škoda. It was dubbed the 3.7 cm KwK 38(t) L/48.7 by the Germans.

The other change concerned radios: the Germans added a tank intercom and an FuG37(t) for the Ausf A–D; this was upgraded to an FuG2 for most tanks and an FuG5 for platoon leaders—standard kit for tank-to-tank communication within platoons and companies—in the Ausf E.

The PzKpfw 38(t) saw action in Poland and in every one of the war's theaters other than Africa—Norway, France, Greece and, of course, during *Barbarossa*. German crews—mainly 7. and 8. Panzerdivisionen—liked them and thought them *"Robuste Fahrzeuge"* (robust vehicles).

The Ausf C benefited from the experience of the Polish campaign and was uparmored, the frontal hull armor increasing from 25 mm to 40 mm. The Ausf D saw 25 mm face-hardened plate added to the existing 25 mm plate, giving 50 mm of protection. The turret armor was also increased—the side to 30 mm, and the rear to 25 mm. Hull sides saw an increase of 15 mm on the upper surfaces. Some of the PzKpfw 38(t) Ausf Bs and Cs were converted into Befehlswagen with replacement radios (for a company commander's tank, an FuG5 transmitter and FuG2 receiver) and the elimination of the hull machine gun.

Panzer 38(t) tanks of Panzerregiment 25, 7. Panzerdivision, near Vilnius, Lithuania, June 1941. The vehicle nearest the camera is an SdKfz 267 which had FuG5 and 8 radios and a large frame aerial. The hull MG was removed, the main gun was a dummy, and the turret was in a fixed position. There were seven PzBef 38(t)s in 2. Pz-Funk-Kp in 7. Panzerdivision's attacks on France and the Soviet Union. Note the marking on the right rear: the map symbol for armored signal platoon. (GF Collection)

A PzKpfw 38 (t) Ausf E/F crosses an antitank ditch in the Rzhev area, July 1942. In the four-man crew, the commander was also the gunner—less of a problem than it sounds because no World War II tanks could fire effectively on the move. In a typical engagement, when the commander spotted a target through binoculars or one of the vision slits, he'd order, "Driver halt! Tank ?00 meters." As the vehicle stopped, the commander would crank the turret round to the required location. Most early German tanks had hydraulic systems; the Pz 38(t) was hand-cranked, as were later German tanks. Soviet and British tank turrets were electrically driven. The commander then shouted, "Armor-piercing shell!" if the target was a vehicle, "HE" if it wasn't, and took aim through the optics. The loader shouted, "Ready!" once he'd loaded the correct round. The commander fired, checked the result, and ordered a reload as necessary.[20] (NAC)

Too small to be upgunned or improved significantly, the Pz38(t) was used as a platform for several Panzerjäger: the Marder III (SdKfz 139) mounting a Soviet 7.62 cm Soviet gun (PaK 36(r)) or 7.5 cm PaK 40/3, the 7.5 cm PaK 40/3 auf PzKpf38(t) Ausf H (SdKfz 138), and the Jagdpanzer 38(t)—today known as the Hetzer (agitator)—of which 2,584 were produced. The PzKpfw 38(t) was also used for heavy infantry guns, the Grille (cricket, SdKfz 138/1) carrying the 15 cm sIG33/1 sIG33/2, and as a Flakpanzer (SdKfz 140), Bergepanzer, Flammpanzer, an ammunition carrier, and training vehicle—although some of the remaining vehicles were also used by Sicherung companies in anti-partisan work in Belarus, Ukraine, and Poland, and deployed as fixed emplacements (*Drehtürme*) in defensive locations such as Norway (75), Denmark (20), France (9), Italy (25), Yugoslavia/ Greece (150), and Eastern Front (78).[21]

Panzer III (SdKfz 141, 141/1, and 141/2)

Crew: All Ausf had a five-man crew of commander, gunner, loader, driver, and radio operator.

The first mass-produced version of the PzKpfw III was the Ausf E, of which 96 were built. In all, 5,690 were manufactured (SdKfz 141: Ausf A–D—70; Ausf G—600; Ausf H—286. SdKfz 141/1: Ausf J—1602; Ausf L—1470; Ausf M—517. SdKfz 141/2: Ausf N—614) between 1937 and 1943, when the production lines were turned over to the StuG III. During that period, the weight of the tank increased from 19.5 tons (Ausf E) to 23 tons, mainly through uparmoring. Additionally, the track width increased to aid floatation.

One of the significant advantages of the PzKpfw III over many contemporary designs was that the size of the turret ring meant that the tank had a three-man turret (gunner, loader, commander), and it could be upgunned from its starting 3.7 cm to 5 cm. Unfortunately, for a tank designed to fight other tanks, its armament was quickly surpassed, and *Barbarossa* exposed its weakness: the gun wasn't powerful enough to defeat the frontal armor of the KV or T-34, even with its final, long 5 cm KwK 39 L/60 version. This meant that while it was the

A PzKpfw III Ausf H(tp)—"tp" for tropicalized—of Panzerregiment 8, 15. Panzerdivision, in the Libyan desert, June 1942. "In tanks, the effects of heat measuring 45°C on the gyrostatic thermometer (113°F) was naturally much greater on the men than among other troops. The heat became unendurable for men in combat, when the hatches had to be closed because of artillery fire and when the engines and ventilating systems had to be shut off during pauses in the action because of the lack of fuel. Nevertheless, the German tank crews held out under even these temperatures."[22] Both sides added extra protection to the front of their tanktrack links (and roadwheels in this case). (GF Collection)

mainstay of the Panzerwaffe from 1939 till 1943, after this time it was relegated to secondary uses, and it was the PzKpfw IV and Panther that saw more widespread front-line use.

The driver was positioned on the left side of the hull front, the radio operator/hull machine-gunner on the right. In the turret, the gunner was on the left with a footrest platform (there was no turret basket), the commander sat under the cupola, and the loader had a fold-down seat at right, although he tended to work standing up—which meant that he had to be careful when the turret was rotated. This was achieved through use of a hand crank. The traverse mechanism was geared, and took either 88 or 132 turns. As the turret turned, so the loader had to follow it.

During the war, the PzKpfw III was uparmored and provided with standoff turret armor and *Schürzen* (side skirts) to protect against antitank rifles. The final version, the Ausf N, saw the introduction of the short 7.5 cm KwK 37 L/24 that had equipped early PzKpfw IVs, and it was used for infantry support.

Sent in numbers to serve in the North African desert, the Ausf G needed tropical equipment, so it had a larger radiator and air filter (although even then the desert sand wreaked havoc with pistons and running gear). On the other end of the climatic scale, the PzKpfw III also had the facility to attach *Ostketten* tracks with extended grousers to help in snow and poor conditions.

During 1943 and 1944, as with other German AFVs, the PzKpfw III was coated with *Zimmerit* paste. This was a prophylactic move to stop magnetic mines or sticky bombs from

Between June and October 1940, 160 PzKpfw III Ausf F, G, and Hs, 8 PzBefWg Ausf Es, and 42 PzKpfw IVs were modified to become *Tauchpanzer*—see caption p. 68. (Bundesarchiv Bild 101II-MW-5674-33)

being attached. (The Germans had just developed a magnetic mine and feared the Soviets would reverse engineer it.) Applied in the field with two coats and a spatula, the paste was hardened with a blowtorch to speed up a process that took about eight days naturally. Unsurprisingly, field application—the coat of paste had to be some 6 mm in depth and added about 220 pounds/100 kg to the weight of a PzKpfw III or IV—was poor and, latterly, factories applied the *Zimmerit* to both tanks and sometimes *Schürzen* before dispatch to the battlefield. However, the process was discontinued in 1944—first, because magnetic antitank mines weren't developed, and second, because there were rumors that it caught fire when impacted by shells. This wasn't the case, but the paste did contain benzene (which could lead to spectacular results when the blowtorch was used to harden it) so there could have been incidents involving unhardened paste.

In 1943 the PzKpfw III also received the improved Fliegerbeschußgerät 42 antiaircraft MG cupola mounting for an MG 34 or 42, and smoke projectors.

The PzKpfw III was used for a range of armored command vehicles, the Panzerbefehlswagen III being termed the *grosse* (larger) as compared to the PzKpfw I's *kleiner*. Of the models used, the Ausf D1, E, and H (SdKfz 266–268) had dummy main guns; the Ausf J (SdKfz 141) and Ausf K versions kept their 5 cm weapons. All the command vehicles had longer-range radios, the SdKfz 266 versions had the FuG6 and FuG2, the SdKfz 267s the FuG6 and FuG8, and the SdKfz 268s the FuG6 and FuG7.

PzKpfw III Auf F on display at the Musée des Blindés in Saumur. Note the *dunkelgrau* color, the *Rommelkiste* (stowage bin attached to rear of turret—first introduced on the Ausf H, it was retrofitted to the Ausf E, F, and G), and 3.7 cm KwK L/46.5 gun. (Igor Kurtukov/Fat yankey, WikiCommons CC BY-SA 2.5 DEED)

PzKpfw III Ausf N of sPzAbt 501 in Tunisia crossing the Medjerda River in Medjez el Bab. The crew appear to be wearing the one-piece overall. Their tropical pith helmets hang from a row of jerrycans, the term for the near-perfect 5-gallon/20-liter liquid containers (*Wehrmacht-Einheitskanister*) which are still used to this day. The cans' colors indicated their content: white = gear oil, red = gasoline, black = diesel, and a large white stripe = water. Today, we assume water was the key commodity in the desert, but as Generalmajor Toppe said, "motor fuel supply was of more importance than the water supply. This is especially remarkable if one compares the required quantities. For example, a tank needs an average of 50 liters [13 gallons] of motor fuel for 100 kilometers [62 miles], whereas, the three crewmembers need only an average of 12 to 15 liters [3 to 4 gallons] of water per day. Added to this is the radiator water, averaging about 7 liters [1.8 gallons]. In a daily run of 100 kilometers, therefore, each vehicle requires 50 liters of motor fuel and 22 liters of water."[23] (GF Collection)

Other variants included the Bergepanzer III—over 150 of which were converted from gun tanks. They had the turret removed, a wooden structure mounted on top, and the crew was reduced to three. There were *Artillerie-Panzerbeobachtungswagen* (SdKfz 143) artillery observation vehicles, *Munitionspanzer* ammunition carriers, *Flammpanzer* (about 100 Ausf M conversions produced the SdKfz 141/3), and a range of assault guns: the ubiquitous Sturmgeschütz III (SdKfz 142, 142/1), Sturmhaubitze 42 (SdKfz 142/2), and Sturminfanteriegeschütz 33B armed with a 15 cm sIG33.

In summer 1940, following the fall of France, volunteers were trained on a *Tauchpanzer* version of the PzKpfw III for deep wading. All openings had to be suitably sealed and fresh air supplied through a 59-foot/18 m long rubber trunk kept on the surface by a buoy. This allowed wading to a depth of 49 feet/15 m. After *Unternehmen Seelöwe* (*Sealion*, the projected invasion of Britain) was canceled, some of the 168 vehicles so modified went east and crossed the River Bug successfully on June 22, 1941.

Panzer IV (SdKfz 161, 161/1, and 161/2)

Crew: All Ausf had a five-man crew of commander, gunner, loader, driver, and radio operator/ bow machine-gunner.

The PzKpfw IV may not have been regarded as the best tank of the war—if such a title could exist—but it was certainly the mainstay of the Panzerwaffe. Some 8,800 were produced from 1937–45: SdKfz 161—Ausf A (35), B (42), C (134), D (229), E (223), F1 (462); SdKfz 161/1—Ausf F2 (175), G (1,275); SdKfz 161/2—G (412), H (3,774), J (1,758). The bulk of these—7,219—were produced from May 1942, after it was realized that the PzKpfw III was unsuitable for upgunning. By the end of the war, more than half of them were the Ausf H model.

The reason the PzKpfw IV became the main German battle tank was because the size of its turret ring enabled upgunning from the original short 7.5 cm KwK 37 L/24 gun of the Ausf A support tank to the long KwK 40 L/43 of the Ausf F2 and L/48 of the Ausf G and later models. This gave the PzKpfw IV an effective antitank role that was particularly important because of the problems the Panther had on its service introduction. The L/48 gun's double muzzle brake improved the single of the L/43; it reduced recoil and allowed increased muzzle velocity to enable penetration of 77 mm of armor at 2,023 yds/1,850 m. In a March 9, 1943 lecture at Hitler's HQ, Guderian said that he wanted PzKpfw IV production to continue at maximum rate as it would be the backbone of the Panzerwaffe. This never came true, partly because of Allied bombing, but also because "Personal struggles for power inside the leadership [which] led to attempts to bypass this order and to phase out the production … in favor of assault guns … to change the offensive nature of the tank arm to the defensive strategy which had become the trend of the last year of the war."[24] Nevertheless, the PzKpfw IV provided the Panzerwaffe with an extremely capable warhorse, and it was the only German tank to be produced and used throughout the war.

The earliest models of the PzKpfw IV—the prototypes built in 1934–35—were introduced into service in 1937–38, but production was reduced once the prewar reequipment program had been satisfied. Experience in Poland led to the improved Ausf E and F models that saw appliqué armor plates increase bow thickness to 2.4 inches/60 mm and hull sides to 1.6 inches/40 mm, increasing the weight to 22.3 tons and necessitating an increase in track width. There were two types of uparmoring: additional armor could be welded on top of the existing armor or it could be bolted or riveted with a space between it and the base armor. The German terms were: *Grundpanzer* (base armor), *Vorpanzer* (appliqué armor), and *Schottpanzer* (spaced armor).

The upgunning of the Ausf F produced the F2 with the KwK 40 L/43 and a redesigned turret with double-flap access hatches, a repositioned commander's cupola, and an increase of weight. The Ausf G, which started delivery in 1942, was notable for the improved double-barreled muzzle brake on the L/43 main gun, and two other important changes: first, the

An Afrika Korps PzKpfw IV Ausf D with 20 mm armor plate added to the front, an external mantlet, and armed with the short 7.5 cm KwK 37 L/24 gun. The insignia on the front left is that of 15. Panzerdivision which surrendered to the Allies in Tunisia, May 1943. The ace of spades might represent a particular company fighting in North Africa. (DZGuymed, WikiCommons)

warning signal light that told the driver that the main gun was overhanging the track width was discontinued; second, the installation of the *Kühlwasser-Austauscher* system for radiator water exchange that allowed one tank to pump hot radiator water to another to help mitigate against the problems of cold weather starting.

The position of the tank barrel was of particular importance to the driver for obvious reasons (if the tank was close to natural features or buildings), but its position over the hatches of drivers and radio operators was also important when it came to exiting the vehicle. All crewmembers in the PzKpfw IV had hatches; there was also an emergency escape hatch under the radio operator's station. Until the Ausf J, the traverse on the PzKpfw IV was by motor or manual hand cranking (190.5 manual turns for a full traverse, as compared to 22.5 seconds for a full traverse using the motor) by either gunner or loader.

The most heavily produced version of the PzKpfw IV was the Ausf H which, compared with the Ausf A, showed the myriad changes that were a result of combat experience over four years of war: the length had increased thanks to the longer gun; armor had increased (the front armor was now 3 inches/80 mm integrally thick rather than requiring appliqué sheets—in the Ausf A it was 0.6 inches/14.5 mm), as had weight (from 18 to 25 tons); and the commander's cupola had been redesigned with vision ports, each a block of replaceable glass. There was a cupola mount for an AA MG, which became increasingly necessary as the Luftwaffe lost control of the air. The side vision ports of loader, driver, and radio operator were dropped— they were pointless with the 0.3-inch/8 mm thick standoff armor skirts around the turret. The gearbox was synchromeshed (except for first and reverse) and the gears were noiseless. There were all-steel return rollers and a strengthened sprocket and idler wheel.

The Ausf H had, however, several drawbacks for the crew. The first, and most obvious, was the lack of vision from within, which was limited to the driver's vision block, gunner's sight, and commander's cupola vision blocks. While they all had protective armored shutters, they were still susceptible to accurate fire from antitank rifles or small arms. The lengthy gun was muzzle heavy, necessitating a compression spring-fitted right segment of the turret ring, and it recoiled 1.9 inch/50 mm further. If it reached 20 inch/505 mm, the recoil indicator

PzKpfw IV Ausf J in the Musée des Blindés in Saumur. Note the "Thoma" wire-mesh *Schürzen* side skirts, and the 7.5 cm KwK 40 L/48 gun. (Igor Kurtukov /Fat yankey, WikiCommons CC BY-SA 2.5 DEED)

Another image of Oberstlt Karl Rothenburg's PzKpfw IV Ausf D (see also p. 26). Note the aerial deflector under the main armament. This was necessary with the short gun to stop the aerial being damaged when the turret traversed. (NARA)

identified *Feuerpause*—a pause in firing. Speed dropped to as low as 10 mph/16 kph because of the extra weight—the suspension could barely cope over rough terrain.

The final version of the PzKpfw IV was the Ausf J, a variant that was characterized by modifications made to speed up production and save on raw materials that were in short supply. This meant that aspects of the tanks which the crews liked were omitted, the most obvious being the deletion of the *Maschinenpistolen Stopfen* (gun ports) on the turret rear

The Tauchpanzer IV submersible tank was created for use in *Unternehmen Seelöwe*. It was used in the Soviet Union by 3. and 18. Panzerdivisionen; this one is seen towing a fuel trailer at the start of *Barbarossa*. Many of the tanks that forged the way in June 1941 towed similar trailers with two (as here) or a single 52.8-gallon/200-liter fuel can. Using trailers or carrying fuel canisters on the back of tanks had its own problems. Apart from the possibility of reversing over the trailers, enemy fire could ignite the fuel and cause the vehicle to blow up. Note the end of the schnorkel at the back right of the turret. (GF Collection)

PzKpfw IV Ausf J during refueling. Each of the jerrycans awaiting use holds 20 l. and a PzKpfw IV will take around 23 of them. (Fotocollectie Spaarnestad Onderwerpen/ Dutch National Archives)

and side access doors, the removal of the vision ports, and the loss of the power traverse. This was canceled in favor of an extra fuel tank that increased fuel capacity from 124 gal (470 l) to 180 gal (680 l), improving offroad range from 134 km to 194 km (80–120 mi) and road range from 188 km to 272 km (120–170 mi). The traverse motor was deleted but the extra fuel tanks weren't initially available when production started in February 1944, and when they did become available, they leaked. It was only in September 1944 that the tanks were reliable enough to insert.[25]

As with the PzKpfw III, the PzKpfw IV had been covered in *Zimmerit* in 1943–44 and provided with *Schürzen*. On the Ausf J, during production, the latter were replaced by cheaper, lighter, wire-mesh panels (*Drahtgeflechtschürzen*) that weren't as heavy, but also weren't as effective (see p. 90).

Some Ausf Js boasted the inclusion of the *Nahverteidigungswaffe* (a close-in defense weapon), replacing external smoke dischargers (*Wurfbecher*), pistol ports, and other methods of close defense against infantry. Smoke pots were damaged or caught fire during fighting; pistol ports weakened the turret structure. So, a roof-mounted system was trialed. It had a 50° tube that mated with a flare gun through a hinged breech and could fire smoke grenades (Schnellnebelkerze 39), IFF (Rauchsichtzeichen orange 160) and other flares (*Leuchtpatronen*), as well as an antipersonnel round (in the Tiger manual named the Sprenggranate-Patrone 326 Lp). This was intended for inclusion on the Ausf H, but appeared too late for this version.

There were many variants of the PzKpfw IV: the *Tauchpanzer* (as per the PzKpfw III), the Panzerbefehlswagen mit 7.5 cm KwK L/48 (SdKfz 141), various assault guns—the Sturmpanzer IV (SdKfz 166 aka *Brummbär*—grizzly bear) armed with a 15 cm StuH43 L/43; the StuG IVs (SdKfz 167 and SdKfz 162); Panzerjäger—Panzer IV/70 (SdKfz 162/1) mounting the 7.5 cm PaK 42 L/70, Hornisse/Nashorn with the 8.8 cm PaK 43/1 L/71; Hummel (SdKfz 165) mounting a 15 cm sFH18/1 L/30 heavy howitzer; various SPAAGs such as Möbelwagen (furniture van, SdKfz 161/3), Wirbelwind (whirlwind), and Ostwind (East wind) I and II; a bridgelayer (Brückenleger IV), ammunition carrier, and *Bergepanzer* (36 conversions between October and December 1944).

Panzer V (SdKfz 171) Panther

Crew: All Ausf had a five-man crew of commander, gunner, loader, driver, and radio operator/ machine gunner.

The Panther was the third most numerous German AFV of World War II: only the production numbers of the StuG III and PzKpfw IV were higher. The Panther was produced in three main versions: the Ausf D (842), A (2,200), and G (2,900 plus). There were also 339 Bergepanthers, the first of these being unturreted Ausf Ds with a three-man crew, with two extra men to operate the winch and crane boom. The Panther also came in command (329) and observation (41) versions (designated *Panther mit KwK 42 L/70 Panzerbeobachtungswagen* with reduced ammunition stowage, allowing the inclusion of extra radio equipment).

The Panther gun tank had five crewmembers: the commander, gunner, loader, driver, and radio operator. The commander, loader, and gunner sat in a turret basket. The two-speed power traverse was supplied by a Boehringer-Sturm L4 hydraulic motor, driven by a secondary drive shaft powered by the main engine. The gunner—using foot pedals—controlled the direction and speed of traverse. The driver sat on the front-left side of the tank, and on the

This PzKpfw V Ausf D Panther is in the Wilhelminapark, Breda. It was given to the city on the first anniversary of its liberation by Polish general Maczek, having been taken from the Krupp testing grounds in Meppen. It left its plinth in December 2003 for nearly a year for restoration by the Wheatcroft Collection. The key differences between this, the first version of the Panther, and the Ausf A that followed, can be seen clearly by comparing this photograph and the one on the next page. First, note on the glacis, the flap through which a machine gun could be fired on the Ausf D and the ball-mounted MG on the Ausf A. Second, the commander's cupola on the Ausf A is higher and has seven periscopes. Third, on the turret side of the Ausf A there is no pistol port; all three—there was one on the rear of the turret and another on the other side—were deleted in this version. (Alf van Beem, WikiCommons [CC0])

other side of the transmission was the machine gunner/radio operator. The radio was an FuG5, the *Panzerbefehlswagen* and *Panzerbeobachtungswagen* having an additional FuG7 or 8.

The crew benefited from excellent optics with the driver, hull gunner, and loader each having their own pair of periscopes. The gunner had a binocular TFZ 12 (Ausf D) or monocular TFZ 12a (other Ausfs) sight and could flip between either a 2.5× or 5× magnification sight. The commander had a panoramic rangefinder sight and a cupola with six viewing ports, each made of 90 mm thick bulletproof glass.

The Panther's escape hatches were good for the driver and the radio operator. They were above their seats but could be blocked if the gun was in the wrong position. The commander used the cupola hatch, as did the gunner—which wasn't straightforward. The loader used the hatch in the rear of the turret.

The design and development of the Panther was rushed from the start. Having thought their medium tanks were as heavy as was required, the first sight of the Soviet T-34 and KV-1 heavies sent shivers down German spines. Armed with a 7.5 cm KwK 42 L/70 main gun, and weighing 43 tons, the Panther Ausf D went from drawing board to production within nine months. The first tanks came off the line in February 1943, and immediately there were teething problems—mainly caused by the fact that the tank was heavier than projected. Hurried into service in time for *Unternehmen Zitadelle*, the results were awful and were made worse by the fact that the units equipped with the new tank—Panzerabteilungen 28, 51, and 52—had had little time to train on them. Indeed, XLVIII. Panzerkorps' war diary for July 2, 1943, said "that deficiencies existed in the Panther units. They hadn't conducted tactical training as a complete Abteilung and radio sets hadn't been tested. Since their assembly areas were so close to the front, permission couldn't be granted for them to test and practice with the radio sets."[26]

Panther Ausf. A turret number 234 was named *Gerda* and is seen in Normandy in June 1944 as part of 2. Kompanie of 3. Panzerdivision's I./Panzerregiment 6. On June 5 the unit was heading east but was ordered back to Normandy and attached to Panzer Lehr. By June 11 it was in action. The attachment of a Panther *Abteilung* to another division wasn't unusual. To work up with a new type, an *Abteilung* would be sent back to a suitable location—one such was the tank-training establishment at Mailly-le-Camp in France—and then return to its division. While it was outfitting, another unit might be attached to the division to ensure it was up to strength. This is what happened with I./Panzerregiment 6. (GF Collection)

Panther Ausf G turret number 332 was part of Pz-Bde 112 when the brigade was destroyed in action with 2e Division Blindée around Dompaire in Lorraine. Captured relatively unscathed, 332 went on to serve in the French Army postwar. Today it's part of the Musée des Blindés collection at Saumur. Note the fresh camouflage scheme and side stowage of equipment, including towing cable and clevis. The main differences between the Ausf G and earlier models were: first, new hull design with steeper sides (to aid production of the Jagdpanther, which would use the same hull); second, deletion of the driver's vision-hatch periscopes and their replacement by a traversable periscope; third, and later in the production run, a new mantlet with a chin to stop rounds deflecting off the mantlet into the hull compartment; fourth, coverings were introduced from June 1944 to help reduce the glow of the exhaust pipes at night. These covers were replaced by *Flammenvernichter* flame suppressor exhaust mufflers from October 1944. (Uwe Brodrecht, WikiCommons [CC BY-SA 2.0])

Zitadelle started on July 5 when there were, nominally, 200 Panthers available. By July 10, there were only 10 operational at the front, although that had increased to 43 by July 13. There were many problems, such as fuel pump deficiencies (56 had burned out beyond repair) and lack of spare parts. The report prepared by Major Mainrad von Lauchert after Kursk highlighted: i) that the taper on the pistol port needed to be strengthened because, were the port to take a direct hit, the cover would be blown into the turret, killing the loader and commander; ii) that roof armor needed strengthening because the mantlet deflected shots down and through the roof into the fighting compartment; iii) 40 Panthers were put out of action by mines, and in one case the mine ignited ammunition under the turret cage—improvements were needed; iv) that training had been too short, which Von Lauchert stressed was the cause of a large percentage of technical and tactical failures; v) the smoke pots were quickly destroyed by enemy fire, and a new way of producing smoke needed to be found.

The main long-term issue was the Panther's operational readiness. Throughout 1943, most Panther units were only able to maintain a 35 percent readiness. Most Panther Ds—as many as 90 percent—broke down with transmission problems within 1,500 km (1,000 mi); third gear was a particular problem, as was the final drive. Fuel consumption was high. The Ausf G wasn't much better.

However, when picking over the problems of the Ausf D's entry into service at Kursk, there had also been one significant success—the gun and optical systems. The Panther crews had claimed 267 kills and the sighting and range had allowed the Panther to pick off Soviet tanks at a distance—the average range was 1,500 m to 2,000 m.

There were two other versions of the Panther: the Ausf A and G. The Ausf A's main visible difference was the ball mounting for the hull machine gun, the reworked cupola, and the inclusion of *Zimmerit* paste. The Ausf G had sloped armor on the hull side plates and deletion of the driver's visor flap (rotating periscopes were substituted). The driver and loader hatches were modified to become hinged types rather than swinging pivot. Later versions had steel

The Panther's suspension and wheel system used the *Schachtellaufwerk* interleaved roadwheel system, which had its pros and cons. The pros were excellent flotation, increased protection for the fighting compartment, and higher speeds over bumpy terrain. The cons were the extra height needed to accommodate the torsion bars running across the hull and the complexity of maintaining wheels that clogged easily with mud and were difficult to access. Note the rubber tires. (Bill Abbott, WikiCommons [CC BY-SA 2.0][27])

roadwheels and an improved mantlet to reduce the likelihood of deflection shots penetrating the crew compartment. This is the version that remained in production until war's end.

The major gun variant of the Panther was the mighty Jagdpanther (SdKfz 173), mounting an 8.8 cm PaK 43/3 L/71 main gun. Three hundred and ninety-two were produced between January 1944 and March 1945. In terms of automotive reliability, it was suspect, but when it did work it was devastating, as the Scots Guards found out to their cost on Mount Pinçon, when three Jagdpanthers from schwere Panzerjäger-Abteilung 654 knocked out 11 Churchills in a matter of minutes on July 30, 1944. Two of the Jagdpanthers were subsequently disabled by reinforcements.

The requirement for a heavyweight recovery vehicle for the Panther, Tiger, and other heavyweights led to the decision that Panther Ausf Ds returned for remanufacture would be converted into the Bergepanther (see pp. 77–78).

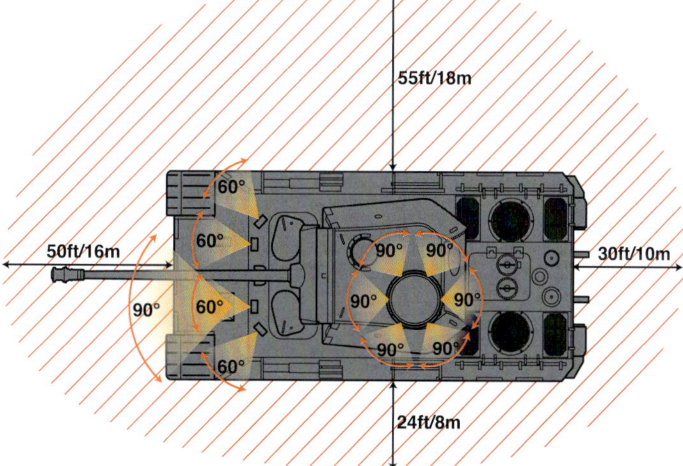

This drawing gives a graphic idea of the restricted fields of view of a Panther Ausf D and the dead zone around it.

Panzer VI Ausf E Tiger I (SdKfz 181)

Crew: five-man crew of commander, gunner, loader, driver, and radio operator/machine-gunner.

Despite it being the iconic German tank of World War II, only 1,347 of the PzKpfw VI Ausf E (Tiger I) were produced between July 1942 and August 1944, when production switched to the Ausf B Tiger II (SdKfz 182). Their effect on the battlefield, however, belied their numbers.

With a design history dating back to 1937, the main stimulus for the Tiger wasn't the shock of meeting the Soviet T-34 and KV tanks: it had been discussed at an important planning meeting with Hitler on May 26, 1941, when Porsche and Henschel were tasked with the production of prototype designs for 45-ton tanks with 8.8 cm main armament in 1942. Henschel's design won, leaving Porsche with 100 chassis built with the expectation of winning the order: they would be used in 1943 as the Ferdinand Panzerjäger, later renamed the Elefant.

With a complicated *Schachtellaufwerk* suspension system that involved layers of interleaved and overlapped roadwheels and a torsion bar suspension system, a combat weight of 57 tons, a Maybach HL210 P45 engine that was changed to the superior HL230 P45, and a deep wading facility (because its weight was too great to be sure of bridges), the Tiger I cost four times as much to produce as a StuG III.

Was it worth it?

There's no doubt that, as a morale booster, it was certainly first class. Allied tank crew knew they would come off second best in a one-on-one fight unless they were very lucky. They cried "Tiger" as often as Aesop's boy who cried wolf. German propaganda made the most of this. Postwar, the cult of the Tiger is even stronger. But even if the claims are accurate and a 5:1 kill ratio is correct—and there are many factors that count against that—the fact is that as a breakthrough weapon, the role for which it was designed, it didn't work. But with Germany on the defensive, the Tigers proved their worth. With an excellent gun—an 8.8 cm KwK 36 L/56 that allowed extreme accuracy—and sufficient armor to provide survivability (something toward which the multilayered roadwheels contributed) and which thus allowed the crew to gain battle experience, Tigers performed better than most other tanks in every way, except for their range and their need

This Tiger has the name *Strolch* (rascal or tramp) under the main gun. The shield with the Baltic Cross (*Baltenkreuz*—as compared to the usual *Balkenkreuz*, bar cross) which is visible on the front bow armor indicates it's from Schwere Panzerkompanie Meyer. Meyer was IC until Hauptmann Schwebbach arrived and, after the latter was killed in combat on January 26, 1944, took command again. (NAC)

for maintenance. Heavy fuel consumption was a problem. So was their weight. If they broke down—and they did, regularly—their weight meant they needed a heavy recovery vehicle and, in its absence, many of these super-valuable vehicles had to be destroyed by their own crews. Possibly as many as 40 percent of the Tigers were destroyed by their own crews—50 Tigers were lost in the retreat from Normandy to the Seine, while only four were lost in combat in this period.[28]

Where did the crews come from? Mainly from Heavy Panzer Replacement and Training Battalion 500, based at Paderborn from early 1942 onwards. Some were veterans, but many were youthful recruits. On one occasion, as recounted in Ganz (2016): "Gefreiter Kurt Nentwig recalled the order that each company of Panzer-Regiment 15 had to detach two crews to man new units: Each master-sergeant was glad about this singular opportunity to get rid of the worst types of all ranks. Months later we saw these '*Blindgänger*' ['misfires' or 'duds'] grinning in brand new Tigers."

Perhaps the best way to assess the Tiger is by seeing what its enemies thought about it:

The design has been well thought out; it embodies several distinctly original features, such as the heavy armament and armor, turret and hull construction, powered traverse layout, and facilities for total submersion ... The PzKpfw VI, with its heavy armor, dual purpose armament and fighting ability, is basically an excellent tank, and despite the defects noted, constitutes a considerable advance on any tank that we have tried.

Its greatest weakness is probably the limit imposed on mobility owing to its weight, width, and limited range of action.

Taking it all round, it presents a very formidable machine which should not be underrated.

Another view of schwere Panzerkompanie Meyer's Tigers, these in Bolzano (or Bozen as the Germans knew it) in August 1943. Note at **1** and **2** the two (of five) *Minenabwurfvorrichtung* launchers visible. This fired a modified S-mine containing 360 steel balls and was used for close-in defense. Its main drawbacks were that it had to be reloaded outside the tank and the launchers were often damaged in combat. It appeared on tanks built from January to late October 1943, when it was discontinued in favor of the *Nahverteidigungswaffe* (close-defense weapon) which was reloaded and fired from within the tank. (NAC)

Above: This vehicle has a problem with its drive sprocket and track, possibly from mine damage. If so, it would probably have needed a crane to sort it out. Note the sun awning above the cupola being put to a different use. There was an attachment for an umbrella in the cupola. (GF Collection)

Schachtellaufwerk

This interleaved roadwheel system gave the Tiger (and other vehicles) a good cross-country ride and low ground pressure to improve floatation, but was a beast to maintain! When it went wrong, if a recovery vehicle wasn't available or a workshop wasn't close to hand, the vehicle would have been destroyed by its crew. Standing orders were that no gun, launcher, tank, vehicle of any kind and no ammunition should fall into enemy hands undamaged. Crew were issued with *Sprengpatrone Zerstörung*—explosive rounds—to destroy the main armament. In addition, another Z85 round was supplied to destroy the engine. Non-combat Tiger losses caused by immobilization for one reason or another were very high, especially during retreats (as in Normandy or from the Dnieper).

Because of the problems with maintaining the wheels, and to save rubber, from February 1944 the running gear was changed. Up till then, each arm had three rubber-wheeled bogies—eight arms with three wheels each meant 24 interleaved wheels, eight of which had to be removed to travel by train. (Frequently, in muddy conditions the front-three bogie wheels were removed to stop the driving wheel jamming.) In February 1944 the outer eight wheels were left off permanently and steel wheels replaced the 16 rubber-tired wheels that were left. This obviated the need to remove wheels for rail transport. When used with the original wider tracks, it made it look as if the vehicle was utilizing *Ostketten* (see photo bottom of opposite page).

Below: Diagram showing the original *Schachtellaufwerk* arrangement for the Tiger and its subsequent alignment. (NARA via Digital History Archive)

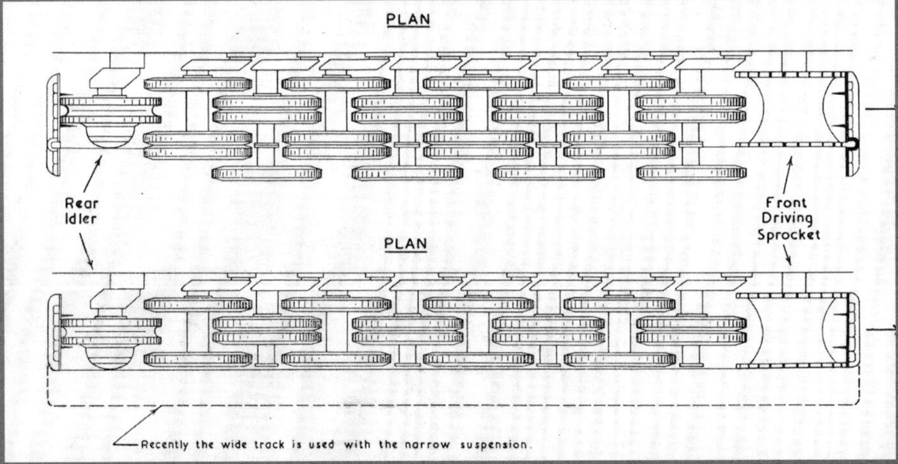

Above: The Vimoutiers Tiger I has sat on the side of the road for many years. It's a bit rusty, but the swivel arm and commander's periscopes can be clearly seen here. The new system gave the tank commander more protection and better viewing options. (TCY, WikiCommons [CC BY-SA 3.0])

Above: Tigers of sPzAbt 503 near Kursk. They were fully committed during *Unternehmen Zitadelle*, with 1. Kompanie attached to 6. Panzerdivision, 2. Kp to 19.PzDiv and 3. Kp to 7.PzDiv. In the attack on July 5, 1943, 2. Kp gets stuck in a minefield and 3. Kp fords the Donets (although one tank bogs). Note the double *Balkenkreuz* symbols on the turret rear. The photograph gives a good view of the "barrel" cupola hatch, which opened vertically, and its locking points. It was later replaced by a lift-and-turn version. (GF Collection)

Below: This Tiger, 213 of 2./sPzAbt 503, is on the Grand Rue of Bourgtheroulde, heading in the direction of Rouen, following the German débâcle at Falaise. 213 has picked up some extra passengers and would be abandoned on the docks at Rouen—sPzAbt 503, having lost all its tanks, was reconstituted in the fall with the Tiger II. (GF Collection)

Stowage

All tanks have equipment stored on the outside of the vehicle. Many have jerrycans or fuel containers, wooden boxes containing groundsheets and blankets for bivvying—or rations and plunder. This example looks at the Tiger I.

Stowage details for the Tiger I, as seen in the *Report on PzKw. VI (Tiger) Model H* produced by the British Military College of Science, School of Tank Technology, Chobham, January 1944. (NARA via Digital History Archive)

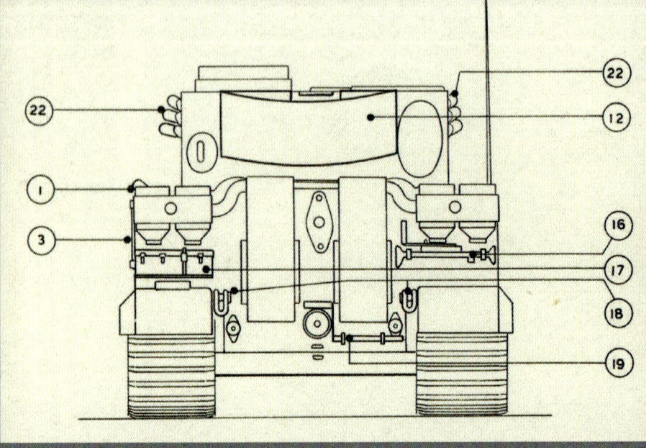

1. Antipersonnel mine attachments.
2. Tow rope.
3. 15 m wire rope.
4. Gun-cleaning rods.
5. Blanking-off plate for air slit engine compartment.
6. Sledgehammer.
7. Shovel.
8. Jacking block.
9. Spade.
10. Axe.
11. Wire cutters.
12. Turret bin (10 track links, 10 track pins).
13. Tetra fire extinguisher.
14. Wireless aerial stowage.
15. Spare track links.
16. 15-ton jack.
17. Track tool box.
18. Towing shackles.
19. Handle for inertia starter.
20. Crowbar 5 ft 10 in.
21. Headlamp positions.
22. Smoke-generator dischargers.
23. Hole for pole supporting camouflage (camouflaged as truck or bus).

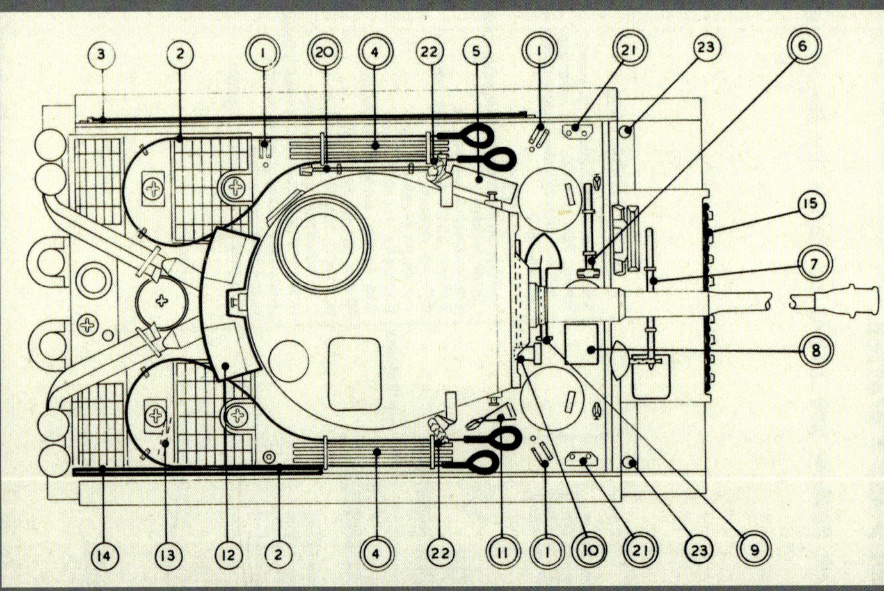

This Tiger is a *Panzerbefehlswagen mit 8.8 cm KwK L/56*—a command tank with a main gun but reduced ammunition stowage (66 rather than 92 rounds) and no coaxial MG. This allowed space for extra radio equipment—in the SdKfz 267 FuG5 and FuG8 radio sets, the latter mounting a *Sternantenne* D (star aerial); in the SdKfz 268, FuG5 and FuG7 sets. Tank II in sPzAbt 503's HQ platoon was originally intended for North Africa, but the unit's Tigers were hurriedly prepared for use on the Eastern Front in early December 1942 and were then sent to the Soviet Union later that month. Note the *Nebelwurfgerät* (smoke dispenser) on the turret side. First mounted in August 1942, these were discontinued from June 1943 after reports of problems in combat. When hit by small-arms fire, smoke was discharged into the turret which incapacitated the crew. (GF Collection)

Tank 312 of the sPzAbt 505, whose "Charging Knight" symbol is on the turret side. Note the swivel commander's hatch and those for loader, driver, and wireless operator. After training at Beverloo, Netherlands, the battalion deployed to Russia rather than North Africa as intended. (GF Collection)

Panzer VI Ausf B Tiger II (SdKfz 182)

489 Tiger IIs were manufactured from January 1944 to March 1945. Upgunned from the Tiger I to a KwK 43 L/71, the Tiger II was heavy (68 tons), underpowered for its size (a Maybach HL230 P30), and cost around RM320,000 to produce, about 25 percent more than a Tiger I. Its drawbacks were obvious: it only had a range of around 160 km (100 mi), and it was too heavy for most European bridges. When Leibstandarte's Kampfgruppe Peiper advanced into the Ardennes spearheading *Wacht am Rhein*, sSSPzAbt 501 went with them. The result highlighted the worst operational problems of heavy tanks: "The hilly terrain in the Ardennes further exacerbated the mechanical difficulties. The soft surfaced, narrow roads were also insufficient for such large, heavy vehicles attempting to move quickly. Peiper realized these deficiencies and considered the Tiger II too slow and too heavy for the rapid advance that was required of his unit. Therefore, he placed the entire battalion at the rear of his column."[29] When Peiper left La Gleize, he left six Tiger IIs behind.

However, when the terrain was suitable—as it was in Hungary for *Unternehmen Südwind*—between February 17 and 24, 1945, sSSPzAbt 501 and sPzAbt 503 (FHH) "led the two corps during the important stages of the operation and only suffered the loss of one Tiger. This was done against a prepared Soviet defense that included 60,000 men, between 100 and 230 tanks and SUs, and over 100 antitank guns."[30]

The upgunned—12.8 cm PaK 44 L/55—Jagdtiger (SdKfz 186) fired two-part ammunition, thus necessitating an extra crewman, the assistant loader; only 38 rounds were carried. It was only employed by two units: sPzJägAbt 512 and 653.

German propaganda labeled the Tiger II the Königstiger, variously translated by the Allies as "King" or "Royal" Tiger.

Tiger II turret 301 of sPzAbt 503 being camouflaged at the Ohrdruf Training Area, Germany, June 1944. The turret man is cleaning the glass vision blocks and the two men at the rear are refueling. Note the 32 mm thick 8.2 m towing cables and cleaning rods. By 1944 the original and unsuitable steel rubber-ringed wheels had been replaced by all-steel ones. These added about 2 tons to already-heavy tanks. The men are wearing the peaked M43 Panzer *Einheitsfeldmütze*. (GF Collection)

PzKpfw VI Ausf B Tiger II demonstrating its ability to cross obstacles and roadblocks in an urban environment—in this case, turret number 200 of sPzAbt 503 in Budapest during *Unternehmen Panzerfaust*, October 1944. 200 was lost in action near Nagykőrös, about 62 miles/100 km southeast of the capital, on November 1 while taking part in the relief force for the surrounded 24. Panzerdivision. The rear-hull plate shows a range of details: the armored exhausts; the covered track-tension points either side of them; a covered starter cover between; and lifting jack underneath. Note also the huge lifting points at the corners of the hull and the jerrycans attached to the turret. (GF Collection)

Funklenkpanzer (radio-controlled tanks)

The Wehrmacht's *Funklenk* (radio-controlled) units were more numerous than many people realize. They used a range of remotely guided demolition vehicles, including the SdKfz 302 and 303 Goliath (100 kg charge, around 5,000 of which were built); SdKfz 304 Springer (330 kg charge, 50 of which were built); and the SdKfz 301 *schwerer Ladungsträger* (heavy demolition vehicle) Borgward IV (450 kg charge, roughly 1,200 built between April 1942 and September 1943). The Borgward IV (BIV) Ausf C could drop its payload at the target and then retreat, allowing multiple uses—although it wasn't well armored and was frequently lost in action, often before it could achieve its goal. Brought to the battlefield by a driver who then exited and used radio control, the BIV had a number of command vehicles, from the PzKpfw III to the Tiger I. The latter was employed by sPzAbt (Tiger/Fkl) 301 (30 Tigers and 66 BIVs); additionally, 3./sPzAbt 504 and 3./sPzAbt 508 each had 14 Tigers and 24 BIVs on strength. By all accounts they were not particularly successful, although they saw

A camouflaged BIV from the Patriot Museum, Kublinka, Moscow **(left)**, and a vehicle captured and tested by the Allies **(right)** showing the detached payload. (Alan Wilson, Wiki Commons [CC BY-SA 2.0 DEED]; NARA)

Char B1 equipping 7. SS-Freiwilligen-Gebirgs-Division Prinz Eugen. Designated the PzKpfw B-2 740(f) in German service, it was used for security work (for example on the Channel Islands) and was converted to carry artillery for use as a *Panzerjäger* or mobile SP gun, in common with so many French chassis. (NARA)

action in various locations: the siege of Sevastapol, minefield clearing at Kursk, at Anzio, ineffectively during the battle of Normandy, and more prominently during the Warsaw Uprising. In spring 1945, 56 BIVBs and Cs were converted into *Panzerjäger* armed with the *Raketenpanzerbuchse 54/1* (see image and caption on p. 7).

Beutepanzer (captured tanks)

The Wehrmacht made great use of the armaments they captured and the industries of the countries they subjugated. As we have seen, Czech industry produced the Pz38(t)—a significant contribution to the Panzerwaffe in 1941—and, later, the Hetzer on the same chassis. Much equipment was captured from the British—at Dunkirk and at various times in North Africa—as were Soviet weapons and equipment during *Barbarossa*. France also provided a wealth of materiel.

Captured T-34s were put to good use—this one by 2. SS-Panzerdivision Das Reich—as the T-34 747(r). It was always a risky business—particularly for air-to-ground, blue-on-blue incidents. (NARA)

Brückenleger II of 7. Panzerdivision's Panzerpioneerbataillon 58 in France in 1940. One of four with the division, it was based on the PzKpfw II. Note behind the first bridgelayer the *Ladungsleger auf PzKpfw I Ausf B* demolition-laying tank that was superseded by the Borgward BIV (see p. 75). (NARA)

Brückenleger (bridgelayer tanks)

The German Army experimented with bridgelaying tanks based on the PzKpfw I, II, and—to carry heavier vehicles—IV chassis. Most had their turrets removed; some PzKpfw IIs kept theirs. They were issued to the bridging units of the panzer divisions but the order for 60 was cancelled after the French campaign. Crew was two or three, and much of the bridgelaying apparatus was manufactured by Magirus GmbH of Ulm.

Bergepanzer (recovery tanks)

An essential aspect of tank warfare was the recovery of vehicles that have been abandoned or which had become bogged or simply broken down. In fact, it was a daily necessity during combat. A key issue here is the fact that often, recovering such tanks needed to be done while under fire—in other words, under the protection of armor. The Germans had a range of vehicles (*Bergungsfahrzeuge*—recovery vehicles), but they were in short supply, particularly towards the end of the war, condemning many otherwise-retrievable vehicles to destruction by their crews.

At first, the German Army used the SdKfz 9 prime mover. Unarmored, this might have worked in the Blitzkrieg years when the army was advancing, but in defense and under fire, as the need—and weight of the tanks—grew, so in 1943 and 1944 the problem had to be solved by converting various tanks to become *Bergepanzer*: specifically, the PzKpfw 38(t) Hetzer (64 tanks converted), II Ausf J (number of tanks unknown, but there was at least one), III (about 150 tanks converted), IV (somewhere between 20 and 36 tanks converted),

One of the few Bergepanzer IIIs, this one with *Ostketten*, passed by men of U.S. Ninth Army in the Rheindahlen area, southwest of Münchengladbach, February 1945. (NARA)

Panther (nearly 350 tanks converted), Bergepanzer VI Ferdinand (three tanks converted), and possibly the Tiger (no exact figures). Some of these specialist vehicles were fitted with the necessary winches, pulleys, cranes, and other equipment, but many weren't. And this figure (at most 600-odd) should be viewed against the provision of vehicles by the Western Allies: 800 M31 Grant and 1,500 M32 Sherman ARVs produced by American manufacturers, let alone those built by the Commonwealth countries.

The Bergepanther was the most numerous version, and most of these conversions produced towing tugs. The actual manufacturing of the Bergepanther required several mechanical innovations: it had no turret and the fighting compartment was filled with the winch and cable drum equipment. A 20 ft (60 cm) metal box was fitted across and around the hull, and wooden extensions added which could be lowered for use as walkways. The winch arrangement, using capstans, could exert a 40-ton pull from a 3-ton effort to tow using a three-piece tower. The spade was raised and lowered by the winch and main cable, and it was locked up for travel. The 1.5-ton jib could lift engines and other equipment.

The trouble was that winches weren't available to begin with, and so many of the new vehicles as well as the conversions were no better than towing tugs. In many cases, the Bergepanthers were not available to retrieve the Tigers when needed. They were too few and too late. In general terms, the Germans were never able to produce sufficient tanks. Specifically, they couldn't provide enough spare parts and recovery vehicles to meet demand. A good example of where having these spare parts and recovery vehicles could have made a difference is the number of Tigers that could potentially have been recovered from noncombat problems.

As far as crewing these vehicles was concerned, the Bergepanzer III had a crew of three (commander, driver, mechanic), as did the Bergepanther. The Bergepanzer IV had only a commander and driver. These numbers may well have been swelled by the inclusion of mechanics from maintenance units and by the assistance of the tank crews from the problem vehicles, if they were still alive. Most vehicles were fitted with an FuG5 radio.

The Bergepanther was designed with a 40-ton internal winch and a 1.5-ton crane boom, but often they were delivered without them. Some had spades to be used as ground anchors; a few of the original Ausf A versions had a 2 cm KwK 38 gun, as does this Ausf G displayed at Saumur's Musée des Blindés. (Alan Wilson, WikiCommons [CC BY-SA 2.0])

Two disabled German Flakpanzer IV Wirbelwinds near Houffalize, Belgium, in January 1945. (NARA)

Flakpanzer (AA tanks)

An increasingly important facet of armored warfare during the war, Flakpanzers were never built in large numbers—the German Army instead had a range of weapons, which were both towed and on SdKfz platforms. The first *Flakpanzer* was the 2 cm Flak 38 auf Panzer I Ausf A. Only 24 of these were built in 1941 and they weren't very good, being used more against ground targets. By 1943, they had all been destroyed.

In 1943, some 140 2 cm Flak 38 L/65s were built on the Czech 38(t) chassis. They entered service in 1944. The single 2 cm gun wasn't particularly effective against Allied aircraft and ended up being used on ground targets.

The main chassis used for Flakpanzers was the PzKpfw IV, which was used for the Möbelwagen (a single 3.7 cm Flak 43, 240 of which were built), Wirbelwind (quad 2 cm Flak 38, roughly 100 of which were converted from tank chassis), and Ostwind (3.7 cm Flak 43, 44 of which were built).

This Flakpanzer IV Möbelwagen is armed with a Flak 43 3.7 cm cannon. The superstructure (see photo on p. 80) has been deployed at the rear but is missing from the side photographed.

This Möbelwagen is in the Musée des Blindés. (Alf van Beem, WikiCommons [CC0 1.0 DEED])

Flakpanzer I of Flak Abteilung (mot.) 614. (Worldwarphotos)

The Flakpanzer 38(t) auf Selbstfahrlafette 38(t) Ausf. M making use of the Czech chassis. (GF Collection)

Ammunition

A significant issue in armored warfare is the provision of the right sort of ammunition, in the right quantities, in the place where it's needed. The Wehrmacht's ammunition supply was complicated by the range of weapons it had—the plethora of *Beute* (booty—captured) weapons and gun types didn't help.

Ammunition production, as with all German production, was dependent on access to raw materials (especially tungsten for APCR rounds) and so was affected by Allied strategic bombing and air interdiction of supply routes. As the German borders shrank in 1944 and 1945, resupply did become slightly easier, but by then shortages were being caused by other factors.

It's true that the German Army had problems with artillery ammunition from the start of *Barbarossa*. Later, during the battle of Normandy, the Allies were able to rain down considerably more shells than the Germans—some sources say the Germans only shelled 10 percent of what the British alone could manage. There were occasions, such as during the Battle of the Bulge, when logistics caused problems with ammunition, but on the whole ammunition—or the lack of it—wasn't a significant factor for the Panzers. What they needed and often didn't have was fuel.

Until the end of 1942, the use of HE and AP with the 5 cm KwK, the 5 cm KwK 39 (L/60), and the 7.5 cm KwK (L/24) was very similar. After this, the numbers changed. Long-barreled 7.5 cm guns were used more in the antitank role, but used less APCR (Pzgr 40) ammunition and more HEAT (*Hohlladung*), possibly because of availability—but this was just as likely to be a tactical choice. The smaller weapons continued to use more HE in infantry support roles.

The range of ammunition included different calibers and different types of shell which were suitable for many, many different guns. This made the loader's job extremely difficult. In the early years and with the early Panzers, a loader's job was cramped and sometimes—in a two-man crew—performed by the commander. It was just as well that these vehicles sported MGs or autocannon loaded by magazine. The arrival of the 3.7 cm gun saw ammunition begin to get heavier and larger and, consequently, the loader's job got more physical—but there's a massive difference between the size and weight of a 3.7 cm main gun round (12 in a box, weight 23 kg, each 15 inches long) and that of an 8.8 cm PzGr 39/43 (each three times as long at 47 inches and weighing 10.8 kg).

Loading ammunition into a German PzKpfw III on the Eastern Front, April 1942. A soldier hands a round to his mate in the tank. It looks black, so may well be a *Panzergranate* AP round. Each ammunition box held two rounds. (NAC)

9. Panzerdivision Ammo Consumption June 1941 to October 1943[31]

5 cm KwK	
APC-HE	24%
APCR	10%
HE	67%

5 cm KwK 39 (L/60)	
APC-HE	39%
APCR	8%
HE	53%

7.5 cm KwK (L/24)	
APCBC-HE	14%
HE	43%
HEAT	38%
Smoke	5%

7.5 cm KwK 40 (L/48)	
APCBC-HE	18%
APCR	1%
HE	34%
HEAT	42%

Left: A fine Josef Arens drawing of a PzKpfw IV Ausf B with its various types of round and drum magazines for the MGs. The Ausf B could carry 80 rounds for its 7.5 cm KwK 37 L/24 main gun. The lighter shells are yellow for HE; the black are AP (see right). Note the radio antenna in its trough; cover over headlamp; front fender hinged back; the visor of the radio operator's vision port is open. (NARA)

Right: The rounds illustrated are *7.5 cm Gr. Patr. KwK mit kl. AZ. 23* = HE round with a graze or direct-action fuze that has an optional 0.15-/0.2-second delay; *Nbgr Patr KwK mit kl. AZ. 23 Nb* = smoke projectile for tank gun using the same type of fuse as 1; *7.5 cm Gr Patr 38 KwK mit AZ. 38* = hollow charge round with an AZ. 38 fuse; *7.5 cm Pzgr Patr KwK mit Bd Zf 7.5 cm Pzgr* = APC tank gun projectile with a base fuse. (GF Collection)

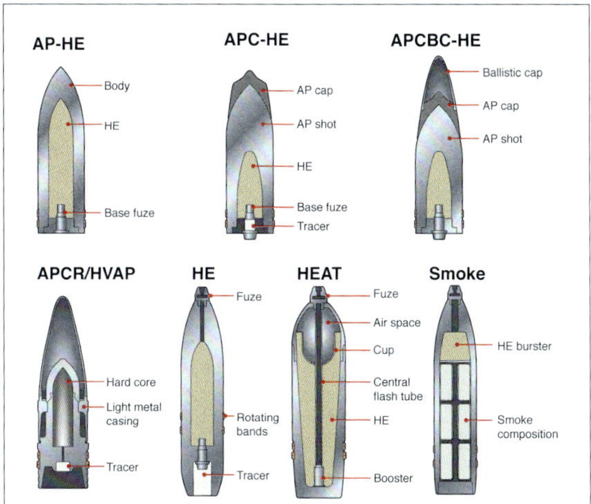

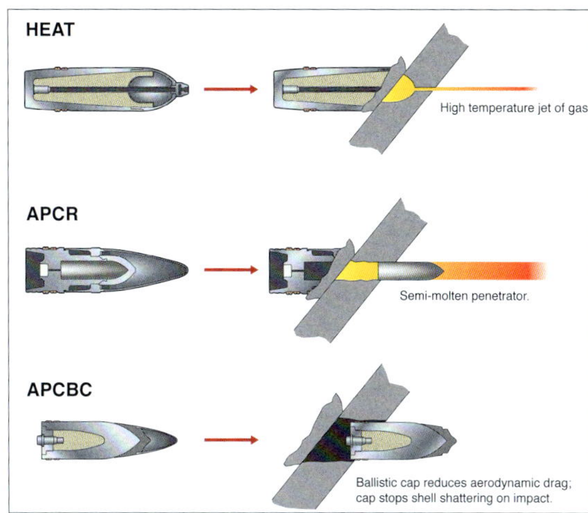

Types of projectile and their penetration of armor.

A page from the German munitions handbook[32] showing the ammunition for the short 7.5 cm KwK 37. The text at left explains the marking of the cartridges:

a) Place, day, month, year of preparation of the round, and identification letter of the firm responsible.
b) Identification figure for explosive type.
c) Weight class.
d) Place, day, month, year of loading, and identification letter of the firm responsible.
e) Company, month, year of filling.
f) Type of gun (more recent rounds bear the inscription: 7.5 cm Kw. K).
g) Weight of propellant.

h) Propellant name.
i) Manufacturing company, year, and delivery number of the propellant.
k) Place, day, month, year the round was manufactured, and the identification letter of the firm responsible.
The drawing below the text identifies the correct key for use with the fuze.

Note: oBD means that the shells do not contain lead, which was used as a decoppering agent (so residue from the firing would need to be cleaned by crew).

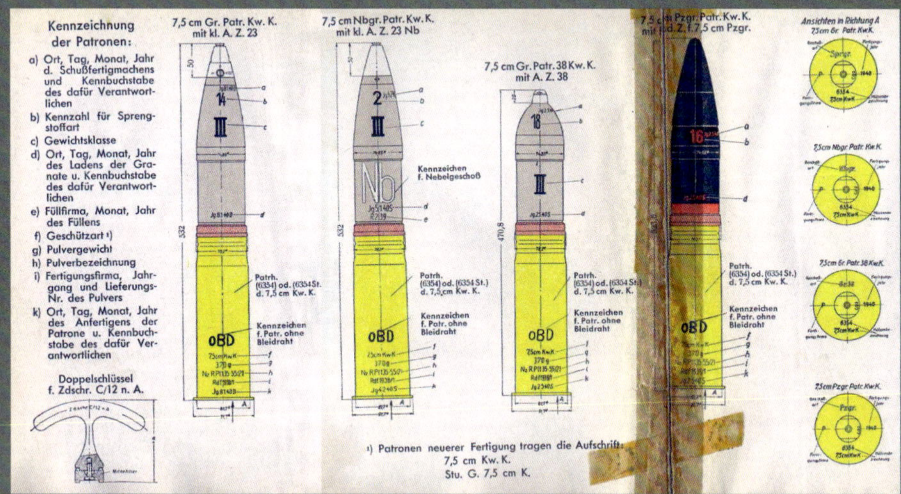

How successful were German tanks in the antitank role? Based on a sample of 12,140 Allied casualties during the war, a 1951 survey[33] identified:

Gunfire exacted the highest over-all percentage (54%) of tank casualties in all theaters …

A study of the average range at which tanks were knocked out by guns or tanks, in all theaters,[34] indicated a figure of 785 yards; the range for hollow charge attack averaged 50 yards for all theaters. …

The site of hits upon tanks immobilized by gunfire was apportioned between the turret, 31%; the hull, 52% and the suspension system, 17%. For hollow-charge attack the equivalent sites were 44% on the turret, 48% on the hull, and 8% on the suspension system. …

The 75 mm and the 88 mm guns accounted for 86% of the total gunfire sample, i.e., 36% and 50% respectively.

Causes of burned tanks, in descending order of incidence, were: gunfire, 65% of which burned; hollow charge, 61%; mines, 21%. …

The German gunners did not seem to have any particular aiming point, unless it was the final drive, and this was just a matter of picking a spot that allowed for a wide margin of error and still assured a hit. Due to the wide dispersal of the hits on American tanks, I am of the opinion that the German gunner fired at whatever part of the American tank that he could see. Most of the American tanks were destroyed by penetrations of the frontal armor, with the hits being well distributed between the front slope plates, final drive, front of turret, and the gun mantlet.

Organized chaos: men of 5. SS-Panzerdivision Wiking load 8.8 cm rounds around the time of the battle of Kursk. (NAC)

Ammunition Stowage

Right: Bucket-brigade. The first man (out of frame) unpacks, the second cleans, the third chucks it up to the man on hull, and the loader stows them in the tank—strenuous work on a Tiger. Note the comparison between the Tiger's 8.8 cm round and the smaller British 6 pdr shell, and also the more severe cut of the SS version of the black Panzer jacket. (NARA)

Left and Below: Diagrams showing ammunition stowage in various Panzers. (Figures identify number of rounds.) In reality, ammunition stowage didn't always reflect the official numbers. The Tiger II, for example, rarely filled the turret bustle because of the danger of explosion if an enemy round penetrated.

Tiger II

PzKpfw IV Ausf E

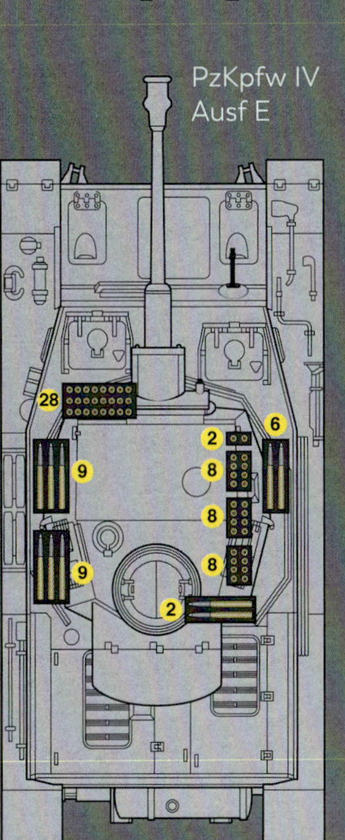

Tiger I

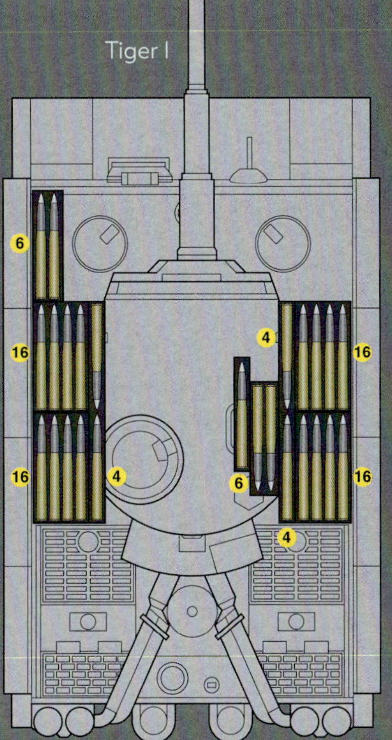

Panther Ausf G

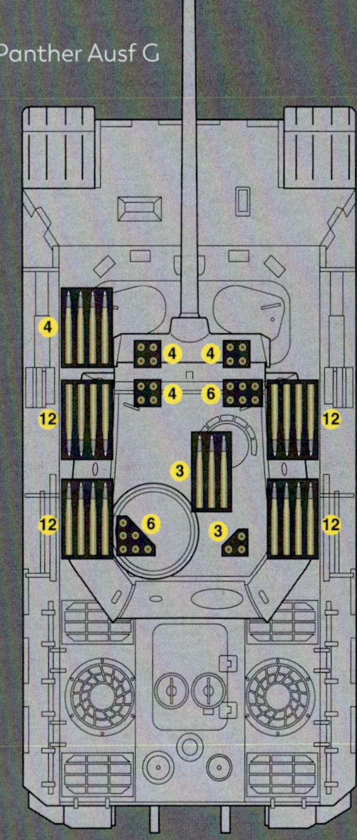

Tank Main Gun Ammunition Types[35]

Tank	Gun	Ammo	Type	Number carried
PzKpfw II	2 cm KwK 30 L/55	Sprgr	HE	180
		Pzgr	AP-HE	
PzKpfw 38(t)	3.7 cm KwK 38(t) L/47.8	Sprgr	HE	42
		Pzgr	AP-HE	
PzKpfw III	3.7 cm KwK L/46.5	Sprgr	HE	131
		Pzgr	AP-HE	
PzKpfw III	5 cm KwK L/42	Sprgr 38 KwK	HE	99[36]
		Pzgr 39 KwK	APC-HE	
PzKpfw III	5 cm KwK 39 L/60	Sprgr 38 KwK 39	HE	84
		Pzgr 39 KwK 39	APC-HE	
PzKpfw III/IV	7.5 cm KwK 37 L/24	Sprgr 34 KwK	HE	56 (IIIL), 64 (IIIM)
		Gr 38 HI/B KwK	HEAT	
		Gr 38 HI/C KwK	HEAT	122 (IVA), 80 (IVB–F1)
		Nbgr KwK	Smoke	
PzKpfw IV	7.5 cm KwK 40 L/48	Sprgr 34 KwK 40	HE	
		Pzgr 39 KwK 40	APCBC-HE	
		Gr 38 HI/B KwK 40	HEAT	
		Gr 38 HI/C KwK 40	HEAT	87
		Pzgr 40 KwK 40	APCR	
		Nbgr KwK	Smoke	
Panther	7.5 cm KwK 42 L/70	Sprgr 42 KwK 42	HE	79 (VD, VA), 82 (VG)
		Pzgr 39/42 KwK 42	APCBC-HE	
Tiger I	8.8 cm KwK 36 L/56	Sprgr KwK 36	HE	
		Pzgr 39/1 KwK 36	APCBC-HE	92
		Gr 39 HI KwK 36	HEAT	
Tiger II	8.8 cm KwK 43 L/71	Sprgr 43 KwK 43	HE	
		Pzgr 39/43 KwK 43	APCBC-HE	72
		Gr 39/43 HI KwK 43	HEAT	

Key to Ammunition Types

Gr Hl   *Granate KwK Hohlladung A/B* = shaped charge round A or B. This is now referred to as HEAT (high-explosive antitank). It uses a shaped charge to fire a jet of molten plasma to pierce armor. The original Gr 38 (without any Hl designation) was introduced in 1940. The Gr 38 Hl/A in 1941, /B in 1942, and /C the year after. Note both Hl/A and Hl/B rounds here are noted FES on the baseplate. This indicates a sintered iron rotating band on the shell to help stability.

Nbgr   *Nebelgranate* = smoke (white phosphorus) round, as distinct from the smoke pots on tank turrets that had a much smaller range. *Intelligence Bulletin* of August 1944 suggests the rounds were used "to achieve surprise, to conceal a change of direction, and to cover their withdrawal. The shells normally are fired to land about 100 yards in front of an Allied force."

Pzgr   *Panzergranate* = armor-piercing (solid shot). This was an important antitank round that came in various forms: APC—armor-piercing (capped)—ammunition has a tip in softer steel, so that when it impacts armor, soft steel *sticks* to the armor and "normalizes"—increases the angle of attack—to help penetration. It's not as accurate as straightforward AP, and the soft cap's aerodynamics reduce velocity. However, it can be married to a ballistic cap that improves matters. The PzGr 39 was just that, an APCBC round but with an added HE-T (and added HE filling and tracer) so that once the shell had penetrated it exploded for maximum effect. The tracer allowed the commander and gunner to follow the path of the round on its way to the target. This was a fixed ammunition round (although different guns would use a version with a different case). The PzGr 40 had no HE filler but did have a tungsten carbide core for increased KE and, therefore, increased penetration. This APCR—armor-piercing, composite, rigid—round (the U.S. Army knew it as HVAP—high-velocity armor-piercing) was the best ammunition for tank killing. Lack of tungsten led to hardened steel being used, PzGr 40 (st) (st = *Stahl* = steel), which was less effective. Even less effective was the PzGr 40 (W), where W = *Weicheisern* = soft iron. After tungsten production ceased in 1944, these rounds were hoarded for use against important targets.

Sprgr   *Sprenggranate* = HE shell, by far the most-used round against everything other than tanks or heavy armored vehicles.

Downward view of the underfloor ammo stowage in Tiger I turret.

Armor

The holy trinity of tank manufacture in World War II, as today, were speed, armor protection, and armament; these are joined by an overall aim towards survivability. Designers soon discovered that if they sacrificed protection, they saved weight and the extra speed could get the vehicle out of trouble, but experience showed that a balance of the three produced the best results. Survivability meant that a knocked-out tank wasn't necessarily destined for the scrapheap, and that some or all of the crew could survive a catastrophe: mines, infantry antitank warfare, tank-on-tank action.

The first building block to aim for was armor protection and, as the accompanying diagrams show, armor thickness altered significantly during the war years, increasing from the PzKpfw I's maximum of 15 mm through to the 185 mm of the Tiger II's mantlet. Armor thickness needed to increase because the enemy's guns and ammunition were improving. As an example, just take the leap made by the British from the early war Ordnance QF 2-pounder (40 mm) that could penetrate 60 mm of armor at 1,400 m using APHV rounds to the late war 17 pounder firing APDS that could defeat 162 mm at 3,000 m.

The other major changes in tank manufacture with an eye to protection were: the use of sloping armor (as can be seen on the Panther and Tiger II), the elimination of shot traps (such as the extension of the Panther's mantlet to stop projectiles deflecting into the crew compartment), and the elimination of pistol ports and other openings in the turret and superstructure.

There were other threats such as the proliferation of mines that necessitated improving the thickness of the driver's armor protection from 6 mm to 40 mm, and the advent of short-range hollow-charge weapons such as the bazooka or the Germans' own Panzerfaust and Panzerschreck. Little could be done to improve armor protection against the latter, but to help protect those vehicles who strayed from the protection of their own infantry, the *Nahverteidigungswaffe* was developed. It could fire smoke shells or a shell/grenade filled with steel balls to clear the area around the tank. As tank-busting aircraft began to dominate the same skies that in the early years of the war had been patrolled by the Luftwaffe, antiaircraft MG mounts were provided, and there was a significant increase in natural camouflage usage—although, as Panzer Lehr discovered at the start of Operation *Cobra*, there was little that could be done against a major bombing mission. On July 25, 1944, 1,600 heavy bombers and 396 twin-engined tactical bombers dropped 3,300 tons of bombs and virtually wiped Panzer Lehr out, knocking out 14 assault guns and 10 tanks.

All combatants used appliqué armor to improve protection in older-model tanks. This is on a PzKpfw III captured in the African desert and shows armor added to the front of the tank around the MG mounting. (GF Collection)

Zimmerit

This was a paste-like coating applied to a tank's body and turret to prevent magnetic mines from sticking. It was composed of 40% BaSO4 (barium sulphate), 25% Mowilith 20—a mixture of PVA (polyvinyl acetate) and benzene, 15% pigment (ochre), 10% ZnS (zinc sulfide), and 10% sawdust. When applied, the benzene evaporated, causing the paste to harden. The deeper it was applied and ridged, the farther away the magnetostatic field. Originally the first layer was factory-applied with the next being built up in the field. It was discontinued in late 1944 due to the mistaken belief that it could catch fire when hit. In reality, it had been unnecessary from the start, as only the Germans used magnetic antitank weapons.

Zimmerit on a Königstiger from sPzAbt 503 in Budapest, October 1944, during *Unternehmen Panzerfaust*. In front a Hungarian soldier talks to a Grenadier of the Totenkopf Division. (GF Collection)

However, there was a disadvantage to this heightened focus on protection: more armor meant less mobility. The result in the design of the Panther was compromise: side-armor thickness was sacrificed to keep its weight down and improve mobility. Crews were aware of this and—as the Allies' tankers did—hung track links on turret sides in the hopes of increasing protection (which didn't work). This weakness was also targeted by Soviet antitank rifle teams. While these ungainly weapons—the PTRS-41 and PTRD-41 14.5 mm rifles were nearly 7 ft long—may have looked old-fashioned, they could penetrate 40 mm armor at 100 m. Used tactically in numbers, their targets were vision blocks, unwary commanders who weren't buttoned up, unarmored vehicles, light tanks with weaker armor, and—if they were close enough—the side armor of most German tanks. *Intelligence Bulletin* of February 1943 reported:

> … antitank rifles have proved effective against enemy tanks. The light weight, portability, and rapid firepower of this weapon permit its crew to go into action in so short a time that it can cover units on the march, at rest, or in battle.
>
> The greatest success has been attained by squads consisting of two or three antitank rifles placed 15 to 20 yards apart. Such units can bring effective fire to bear on a target, and have a greater chance of putting it out of commission than fire by a single rifle would have.

Such was the success of these antitank rifles that the Germans had to respond—and their response has led to a misinterpretation that persists to this day. The adoption of *Schürzen* was as a direct result of these rifles rather than—as is sometimes maintained—

This captured PzKpfw III Ausf L shows the yawning gap above the roadwheels that was targeted by Soviet antitank rifles. Note also spaced armor on the gun mantlet and on the hull front, the escape hatch between the front two return rollers (deleted later in the production run), the so-called *Rommelkiste* stowage bin on the back of the turret, and the open turret hatches. (Battlefield Historian)

Closeup of the *Schürzen* on a PzKpfw IV Ausf G of the 2. SS-Panzerdivision Das Reich southeast of Kiev, December 1, 1943. (GF Collection)

Closeup of the wire ("Thoma") *Schürzen*. (NARA)

as a defense against bazookas or other hollow-charge weapons.[37] Their placement on the Panther in particular covered the space between the roadwheels (which provided their own protection) and the sloped armor sides. The extra weight of the *Schürzen* was later reduced using wire screens—the so-called Thoma screens.

As Germany's conquests were reclaimed by the Allies and the sources of raw materials vanished, German manufacturing was affected. This was especially true when it came to ammunition. That tungsten was in short supply meant fewer rounds using a tungsten penetrator were produced. However, the effect of the encroachment of the Allies on the manufacture of armor is less well documented. American postwar tests on Panthers (using a 90 mm gun) and British tests on a Tiger have been used to document the lower quality of the armor of some late-war vehicles, specifically the lack of face-hardening. The British test report[38] said:

> The fact that the armor is no longer surface hardened, and has a relatively low Brinell hardness, is very important. It must be noted that this change coincides with the appearance of new German heavily armored tanks: Tiger, Panther, Ferdinand. Until now, no German tank had armor thicker than 50 mm. … The [Tiger, Panther, Ferdinand] were built for the purpose of long-ranged combat. It is possible that the enemy introduced softer armored vehicles knowing that the Allies use armor-piercing capped shells. Use of these shells against soft armor is suboptimal. If soft armor continues to be used, we must explore the question of ballistic caps. However, it is necessary to collect more information, as this armor could still be surface hardened.

However, others (notably Jentz and Doyle[39]) suggest this may not have been the case: "There is no proof that substandard German armor plate was used during the last years of the war. All original documents confirm compliance with standard specifications throughout the war."

The fact is that homogenous armor (layered rather than case-hardened armor) was more resistant to the capped rounds that the Allies brought in after experience in the field (mainly in North Africa) showed that their uncapped shells broke up on impact with the German case-hardened armor. And even if the Germans were low on molybdenum—which the Tiger I (though not the Tiger II) had it in its steel—and tungsten, what they really needed was fewer air raids and more spare parts.

The method of affixing *Schürzen* is well illustrated in this view of an observation tank variant of the PzKpfw IV, in this case converted from an Ausf J recovered in Belgium. Similar to a standard Ausf J, the Panzerbeobachtungswagen IV carried the same 7.5 cm KwK 40 L/48 main gun. These observation tanks were used by artillery and had an improved periscope and three radios, two (FuG4 and FuG8) in the turret and the usual FuG5 position in the hull. Note the AA gun mount (*Flieger-Beschußgerät für MG-34*) and the *Turm-Sehrohr 1* stick periscope with a ball mount in the turret top. These PzBeobWg IV vehicles were used with Wespe and Hummel units. Ninety were converted to this variant between July 1944 and March 1945. (NARA)

Crew Duties and Positions

World War II tanks were complicated and sophisticated pieces of machinery. More than any other motor vehicle, these tanks were subject to defects. Some part was always in need of attention, even if it was only a loose nut or bolt that needed tightening. For this reason, the drivers as well as the tank crews were instructed to constantly check even apparently serviceable tanks for defects and repair them immediately.

Keeping tanks on the road, fighting in them, and commanding them are all difficult enough tasks individually, but when these duties have to be combined, life gets very difficult very quickly. The problem with the early Panzers was that they were small and so they had to have fewer crew, meaning these crewmembers had to multitask. The commander in both the PzKpfw I and II doubled up as gunner; in the PzKpfw II, the loader was also the wireless operator. For the PzKpfw 35(t) and 38(t), the Germans removed ammunition stowage to provide room for a fourth crewmember to reduce the commander's duties (in the three-man version, the commander loaded and fired the gun as well).

When it came to the next generation of tanks, the Germans ensured that they were roomy enough to have a five-man crew. This meant the commander commanded and didn't have to worry about loading and firing. It meant that there could be an even and specific allotment of duties. Each crewmember was dependent on the others: fighting in a tank was very much a team effort.

Ranks were, of course, important—they always are in any army—but within a tank unit, much of the starchiness apparent in prewar barracks went by the board. The upper echelons of a regiment or *Abteilung* would consist of officers; troop commanders could be junior officers or *Unteroffizier* (warrant officers or senior NCOs); tank crew could be anything from trooper to sergeant. Soldiers worked their way up the ranks—the famous

Some jobs needed the whole crew's involvement. Here, a PzKpfw III Ausf H is raised by a 5-ton jack for link replacement or repair. The turret man appears to be holding a track-linking tool to hold the two ends together to allow the joining pin to be hammered in. Note crowbar to the right and a winch frame to the front. (NAC)

Crew Seating Positions

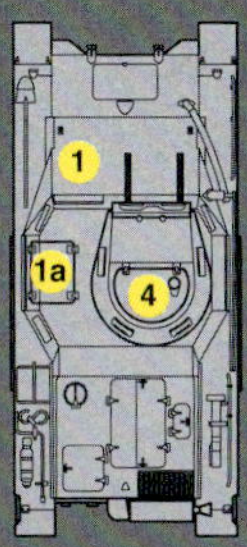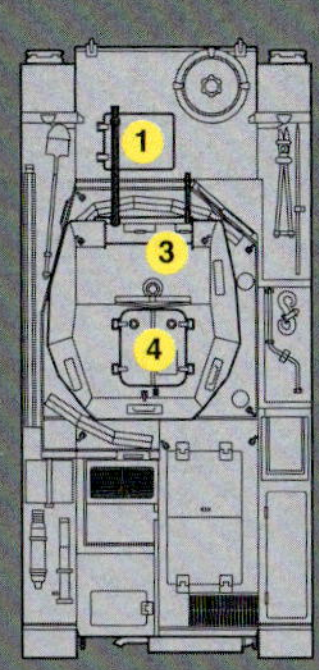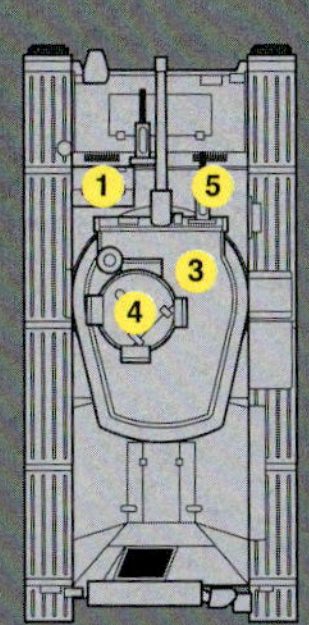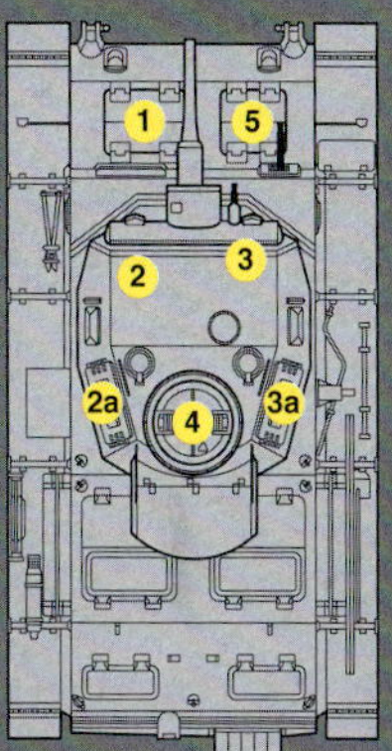

Diagrams showing crew seating positions and hatches for: above, L–R—PzKpfw I, PzKpfw II, PzKpfw 38(t), PzKpfw III; below, L–R— PzKpfw IV, Panther, Tiger, and Tiger II.

Key: 1 and 1a Driver and hatch; 2 and 2a. Gunner and hatch; 3 and 3a. Loader and and hatch; 4. Commander; 5. Radio operator/bow gunner.

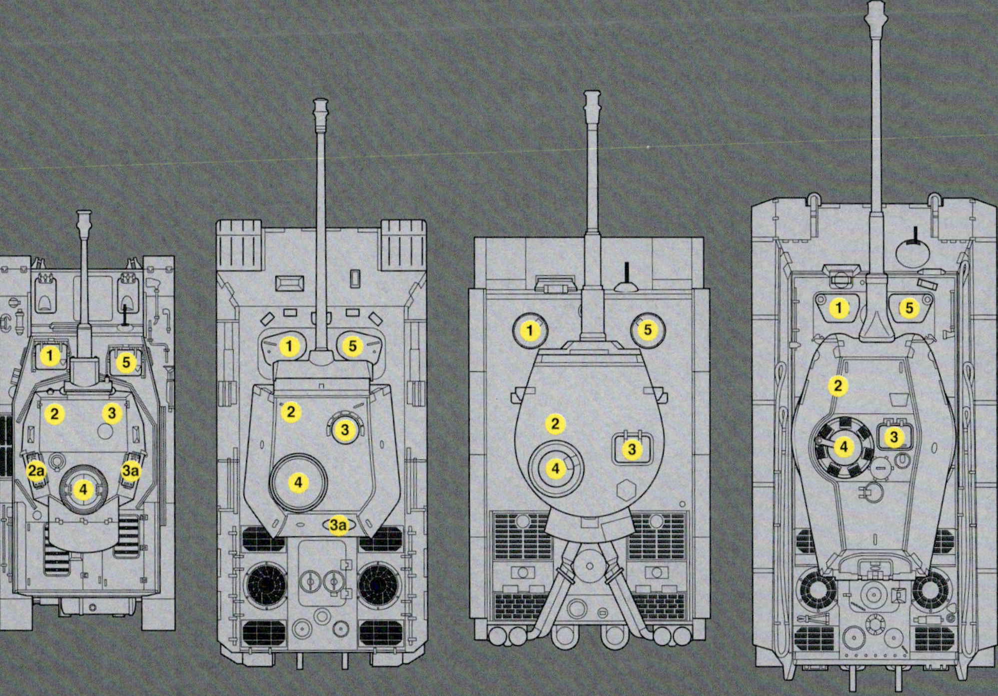

Michael Wittmann, for example, started the war as an *SS-Unterscharführer* (corporal) but died an *SS-Hauptsturmführer* (captain). Otto Carius—who claimed more than 150 tank kills—left school in 1940 and started off as a loader after having been rejected as unfit for military duty (he was, apparently, underweight). He started as an infantryman, volunteered for the Panzers, and ended the war commanding a Jagdtiger company as an *Oberleutnant* (lieutenant).

The reader should remember that every tank was different and had different vision devices and systems. What all tanks did have in common was that they were cramped, noisy, either very cold or very hot, and often smelly given that in combat, attending to calls of nature meant making use of ammunition boxes, expended shell cases, or any suitable receptacle. The crew compartment was filled with the smoke of battle: engine fumes, fumes from firing the gun, and fumes from those receptacles.These were the basic duties of the crewmembers:

Commander (**Panzerführer** *or* **Panzerkommandant***)*

Usually a sergeant, unless part of the upper echelons of a unit, the commander nevertheless was "the boss" when it came to his tank—although tanks and crews changed regularly for various reasons, including combat. The commander chose the tank's targets, selected the ammunition type to engage, directed the tank, and communicated with other commands. He was responsible for crew welfare, motivation, and training, training, and training. How he was regarded by the crew—and others in his unit—was crucial in making a good, cohesive team … or not.

The commander had several options as to where to position himself in the turret. This depended on the vehicle he was in, and whether the tank was in combat or in a dangerous area. In the case of the latter, the commander could sit or stand in the tank "buttoned-up"—with all the hatches locked, using his vision devices to control the tank and its targets—or could command from a head-out position. This was vastly more dangerous—particularly as tank crew rarely wore helmets because of the spatial restrictions and problems wearing helmets with headphones. He'd keep his head down as far as he could and use a "donkey-eared" periscope to look over the turret rim if things were dangerous.

Panther commander (5. SS-Panzerdivision Wiking) using his turret periscopes. At A is the rod connecting the turret ring to the commander's azimuth indicator (the *Gelenkwelle zum Antrieb de 12-Uhr-Zeigers*). The *Richtschütze* had one too, so that both men could work in harmony, and so that when target positions were given (one/two/three o'clock, etc.) both men were looking in the same direction. (NAC)

Above: PzKpfw IV Ausf G *Richtschütze's* station. Note **1** monocular sight, **2** elevating handwheel, **3** traverse handwheel, **4** breech of 7.5 cm KwK 40. The curved metal at right is the deflector guard that ensured spent cases were ejected away from the *Richtschütze* and the commander. (GF Collection)

Right: Panther *Richtschütze* using his sights. (NARA)

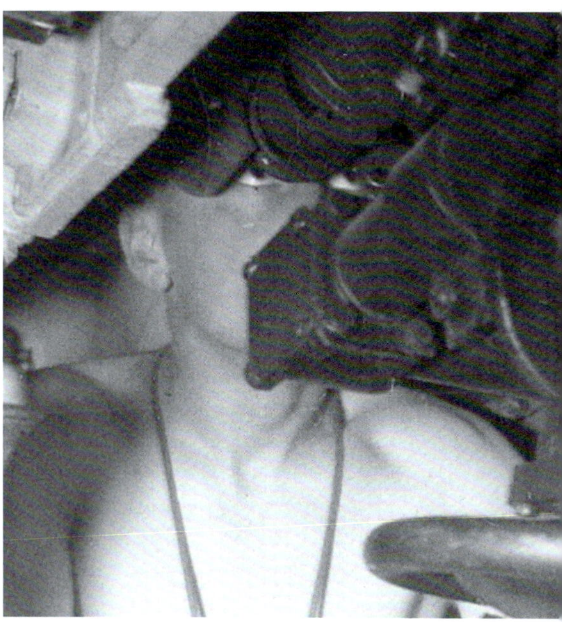

In a Tiger I, the commander had a shield on his right to protect him from backflash from flashing ammunition. His vision devices were made watertight with rubber seals. The glass blocks and prisms were easily changed, and spares were carried. This was just as well, as they were targeted by infantrymen, and on the Eastern Front by Soviet antitank rifle squads.

Gunner (Richtschütze)

The gunner operated the turret, laid the gun to engage the target, and—most importantly—kept calm. He was the assistant commander and a potential commander in his own right. Balthasar "Bobby" Woll, Michael Wittman's gunner, is said to have destroyed 80 tanks and some 107 antitank guns, along with numerous other vehicles. He was awarded the Knight's Cross of the Iron Cross, and was the only tank gunner to receive this award. While the commanders tended to get the glory, the gunner was the man who engaged the enemy.

Loader (Ladeschütze)

First and foremost, the loader had to make sure that he could lay his hands on the type of shell his commander ordered—something that got more difficult as time went on and the range of ammunition options grew. (See section on ammunition and ammunition stowage pp. 81–8.)

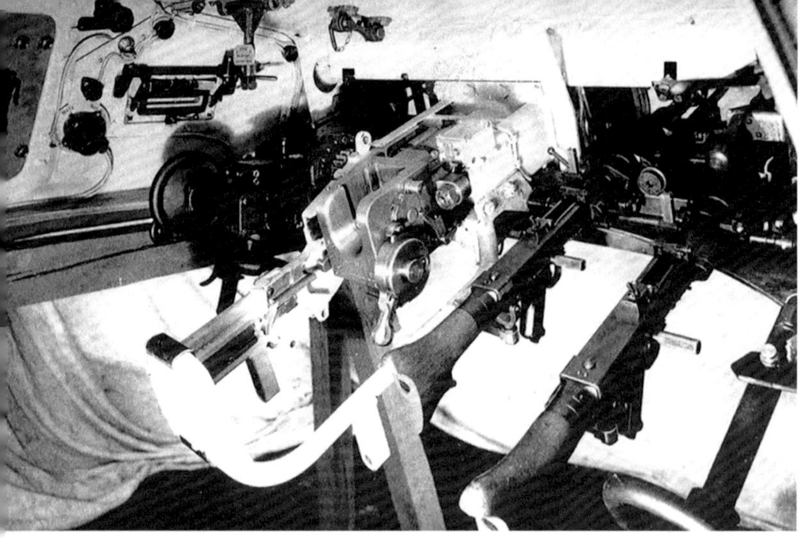

PzKpfw III Ausf A showing *Ladeschütze*'s position with double MGs and 3.7 cm KwK L/46.5 main gun. Note the left and right traverse handwheels and *Richtschütze*'s vision port. (GF Collection)

Panzer IV Ausf E looking across the *Ladeschütze*'s position and coaxial MG to the 7.5 cm KwK 37 L/24 main gun. Compare the breech size to the 3.7 cm of the PzKpfw III Ausf A. In the roof above the coaxial MG is the fume ventilator, a modification on this *Ausführung*. (GF Collection)

PzKpfw IV Ausf G *Funker*'s position. Note MG mounting vision port at right, sight, and the cramped conditions. (GF Collection)

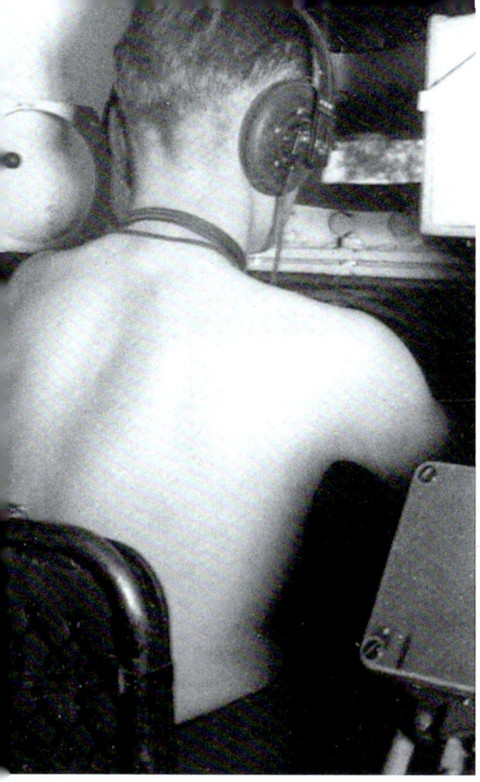

Panther *Fahrer* showing his vision slit. (NARA)

To feed the gun, strength and speed were essential. The loader also had to fire the coaxial MG if there was one. Specialist training was not needed, but in tanks without a turret basket (such as the PzKpfw III) the loader had to walk as the gun traversed.

Driver (Fahrer)

The driver focused on driving and following orders, and was the most likely to get extra rest when the opportunity arose. Peering through his vision devices, he had to trust in his commander for instructions but, wherever possible, find the best and safest route. For the driver, there would be no such thing as rest if the tank had mechanical problems; the driver was key to getting the vehicle back into service.

Radio Operator (Funker)

Wolfgang Schneider's excellent *Panzer Tactics* sums up well the position of *Funker* in a Panzer crew. On the one hand he was "an 'intelligent' soldier … capable of handling delicate equipment." On the other, he was "*Stullenmax*"—a "gofer" who did many of the mundane chores (laundry, meal preparation, housekeeping).

In fact, the role of *Funker* was crucial to the tank, particularly in action. Having good communications within the tank, with troop, *Abteilung*, and *Regiment*, was essential to command and control of the minute-by-minute, second-by-second tactics that were the difference between life and death. And when the *Funker* wasn't doing that, then he could fire the bow machine gun.

Most German tanks would have had a radio for communication with other tanks in the *Zug* or *Abteilung* (often an FuG5; see below); command vehicles would also have had an extra radio so one could be used for receiving and one for transmitting.

Armored Force Communications

As explained in *TM-E 30-451 Handbook on German Military Forces*, March 15, 1945:

a. GENERAL. Complete sets in armored vehicles include transmitter, receiver, power units, and accessories, referred to by the designation Fu., followed by a number. An exception is the voice transmitting set Fu. Spr.f. used in self-propelled field and medium artillery vehicles and certain armored cars. This set has no Fu. number. Transmitters and receivers individually are referred to by a description and a letter, such as 10-watt transmitter "c".

b. RADIO SETS USED. The following tabulation shows what complete radio sets are likely to be installed in various types of armored and self-propelled artillery vehicles.

Main Panzer Radio Equipment

Vehicle	Radio
Commander's tank	Fu.8 and Fu.5; or Fu.7 and Fu.5
Fighting tanks, all types	Fu.5 and Fu.2; or Fu.5 only
Assault guns (in armored formations)	Fu.5 and Fu.2; or Fu.5 only
Armored OP vehicles (artillery)	Fu.8 and Fu.4; or Fu.8, Fu.4, and FuSprf.
Assault guns (artillery)	Fu.8, Fu.16, and Fu. 15; or Fu.16 and Fu.15; or Fu.16 only
Self-propelled antitank (light and medium chassis)	Fu.8 and Fu.5; or Fu.5 only
Self-propelled antitank (heavy chassis)	Fu.8 and Fu.5; or Fu.7 and Fu.5; or Fu.5 and Fu.2
Antitank-assault guns	Fu.8 and Fu.5; or Fu.5 only
Lynx (reconnaissance)	Fu.12 and FuSprf. or FuSprf. only
Antiaircraft tanks (Flak panzer)	Fu.5 or Fu.2 only
Self-propelled heavy infantry gun	Fu.16 only
Wasp and Bumble Bee	FuSprf. only
Armored cars (except eight-wheeled vehicles) and semi-tracked vehicles with armament	FuSprf. only or Fm.22 and FuSprf.
Eight-wheeled armored cars	Fu.12 and FuSprf. or FuSprf. only

Panther *Funker*'s position showing the FuG5, one of the standard Panzerwaffe radios. The bow machine-gun sight is obvious, as is the head pad (at top) with which he could move the gun. (GF Collection)

Access Doors and Escape Hatches

Knowing you can get out of a tank that has been hit, is on fire, or is in in some form of distress (sinking in a bog, in a river after falling through a bridge, etc.) is an important factor for crew morale. Most German tanks (the PzKpfw IIIs and IVs) had turret-side access hatches, as well as the commander's cupola, and sometimes hatches in the glacis/hull top for driver and radio operator; in other cases, they had escape hatches in the hull sides above the wheels (PzKpfw III Ausf D to Ausf L partway through production run). Other tanks had more difficult routes to safety and included hatches under the tank (not ideal if the problem involved water) and in some cases, crew had to make their way through the commander's cupola. The Panther and Tiger had hatches in the rear of the turret.

Above right: *Funker* leaning out of the circular escape/entry hatch at the back of a Panther Ausf D Panther. (Note older type commander's cupola.) He has headphones with a throat mike, allowing him to communicate within the tank via the Panzerkosten 20 system. (NARA)

Right: The proximity of the crew to each other is well seen in this Panther Ausf A turret view. Note the later cupola with the mount for an AAMG at right. (NARA)

Below: The PzKpfw III and IV had side-turret access/escape hatches. They were single- or double-doored depending on variant (this one has double). They came with a vision port, **1.** Note also Ladeschütze's turret vision port at **2.** This form of commander's double-hatched cupola **3.** was used on several Ausführung of the PzKpfw III and IVs. (GF Collection)

Panther *Fahrer* in the direct vision position. Note the two periscopes used when the hatch was closed. See also drawing on p 67. (NARA)

Camouflage

Originally the Panzers were produced in dark gray, but it soon became clear that they needed to be camouflaged. The colors and patterns were carefully set out, some being applied by the manufacturers, others in the field. Inspectors ensured the consistency of paint production and its application at the factories, but the exigencies of war and fact that sufficient quantities of paint were not always available meant that there was often a lack of consistency. This was made more variable in the field by the effects of climate, weather, usage, and different means of application, etc. The main camouflage colors used were:

- *Dunkelgrau* nr 46 (RAL[40] 7021) (dark gray)
- *Dunkelbraun* nr 45 (RAL 7017) (dark brown)
- *Elfenbein* (RAL 1001) (ivory)
- *Gelbbraun* (RAL 8000) (yellow brown)
- *Graugrün* (RAL 7008) (gray green)
- *Braun* (RAL 8020) (brown)
- *Grau* (RAL 7027) (gray)
- *Dunkelgelb nach muster* (RAL 7028) (dark yellow according to pattern)
- *Rotbraun* (RAL 8017) (red brown)
- *Olivgrün* (RAL 6003) (olive green)

At first, all Wehrmacht vehicles were painted in dark gray. Between 1939–40 a secondary color (*dunkelbraun*) was added, although it dropped out of favor and the Wehrmacht reverted to the original scheme. From 1943, *dunkelgrau* was dropped in favor of *dunkelgelb*, with secondary colors of *rotbraun* and *olivgrün*, the latter tending to be the color most often used in the last months of the war. Two more complicated styles of camouflage were often used in the last years of the war: *Hinterhalt-Tarnung* (ambush camouflage) and *Splittermuster*

The Panzer III Ausf F at Saumur—Red 125—was built in Berlin, leaving the Daimler-Benz factory in July 1940. It had been uparmored—*Zusatzpanzerung*—before it left. It's camouflaged in the early war *dunkelgrau* and its turret number indicates that it is the fifth tank in 1. Kp's 2. Zug. (SF)

Sitting outside the December 44 Museum in La Gleize is Tiger II; and Königstiger 213 from sSS-Panzerabteilung 501, the platoon command tank of SS-Obersturmführer Dollinger. It was part of Kampfgruppe Peiper. On December 22, 1944, two Königstigers—213 and 211—fought Shermans of Task Force McGeorge. Both were disabled: 211's traverse mechanism and 213's gun were severely damaged by direct hits. Both tanks were abandoned. 213 owes its current paint scheme to a 1994 restoration, owing to which its missing side and rear fenders were also restored. (GF Collection)

(splinter pattern). Ambush employed extra spots on the three colors: green and brown on yellow, brown and yellow on green, and green and yellow on brown. Splinter used the colors in sharp-edged regular stripes.

Several other requirements affected camouflage schemes. First, the attack on the Soviet Union meant that winter of 1941/42 saw the need for suitable snow camouflage. This was applied in the field using whatever was available, whitewash and chalk being most frequently used. These schemes tended to fade or flake off through usage.

In 1941, German tanks were sent to North Africa for the first time, and the desert war brought with it its own camouflage necessities. From the start, *gelbbraun* was the most used color, with *graugrün* being the second most used. It became necessary to change this in 1942, when *braun* became the primary and *grau* became the secondary. An interesting observation on camouflage in the desert was made by Generalmajor Alfred Toppe postwar:

> Camouflage is very difficult in the desert and, in many cases, impossible. "During the day, it was impossible to camouflage the movements of troops and columns from air observation. In the neighborhood of the front, the troops could only with difficulty be camouflaged from ground observation. The unavoidable dust clouds they raised betrayed any movement."[41]

The three colors used after 1943—*dunkelgelb*, *rotbraun*, and *olivgrün*—were used to produce *Hinterhalt-Tarnung*, the famous ambush camouflage. This saw random patches of *rotbraun* and *olivgrün* painted over *dunkelgelb*, with spots of the yellow applied over the other two colors. Various factories were involved in this, such as Daimler-Benz, MAN, and MNH (the main three Panther manufacturers), Demag, Henschel, Krupp, Nieblungenwerk, and Škoda. Daimler-Benz produced the so-called dot style for the yellow spots; MAN and MNH produced a disc version. Tank interiors were usually painted *elfenbein* or *graugrün*.

Above left: This late-production PzKpfw IV Ausf J of 10. SS-Panzerdivision Frundsberg is camouflaged in *Hinterhalt-Tarnung* (ambush camouflage)—note the characteristic dots—and wire-mesh skirt *Schürzen*. The crew of the Panther opposite have broken up the horizontal outlines of the tanks with whatever was to hand. Breaking up the outline of a vehicle by using vertical strips—timber, doors even—was a commonly used technique, as was using soil or mud. (NAC)

Above right: Crew camouflage Tiger 222 of sPzAbt 502 with white paint. Note the one-piece overall—popular because it didn't need a belt which sometimes caused snagging problems in the vehicle—and the smoke dischargers. Because there were problems with them in firefights, they weren't installed after July 1943 and many had them cut-off in the field. (GF Collection)

As well as paint, natural camouflage—particularly foliage—became increasingly part of the tanker's remit as Allied Jabos began to dominate the skies. Shown here are foliage-camouflaged Panther Ausf As in the Moselle Valley, October 1944. Postwar analysis of the Allied air forces' claims shows that very, very few German tanks were knocked out from the air. Nevertheless, they harassed the Panzers and destroyed thousands of other vehicles and supplies to make movement in daylight very difficult for the Germans. (NAC)

Mobility

One of the keys to the success of Blitzkrieg was the ability to move large amounts of men and equipment quickly. After suitable reconnaissance had taken place, each division was given a designated road or sector of advance. The commander with overall responsibility for control of the march and regulation of traffic was usually near the head of the main body. The column was organized into a *Vorhut* (an advance guard), *Gros* (main body), and *Nachhut* (rear guard). The *Vorhut* had important functions. It reported enemy locations and obstacles such as minefields, and had an accompanying *Pionier* unit to repair roads and bridges as necessary and place route markers. The task of road maintenance sometimes became the responsibility of the division engineer officer, although often it was performed by service troops who became extremely proficient at it and were assigned to these duties repeatedly.

Times were calculated to prevent traffic congestion. An armored division's average march was 60–90 miles a day. To ensure this was strictly adhered to, a traffic echelon was established, usually with: a *Stabsoffizier für Marschüberwachung* (staff officer for traffic control); the "Stoma," who had complete control; a team of traffic control personnel (in red-orange brassards); and MPs (the *Feldgendarmerie* in their distinctive metal gorgets). Air observation could also be used.

During the war, this setup was made permanent and became the responsibility of the G-3/Traffic Regulation and Control Office (TRACO). During a movement, the TRACO exercised jurisdiction over all the troops involved in completing the movement: MPs,

Repair of mine damage to a PzKpfw III Ausf J tank of 1. Panzerdivision (note the divisional marking on hull side near bow machine gun) in July 1942. Mines were more likely to disable the tank than to kill its crew. (NAC)

Feldgendarmerie were soon armed exclusively with submachine guns. They often had to be issued with cold rations because of the far-flung nature of their employment. They needed maps, painting and sign-making equipment, and were identified by their gorgets—which led to their nickname, the "chained dogs." (RCT)

motorcycle messengers, interpreters, supply personnel, signal troops, engineers, scouts, medical personnel, and other combat support elements. The TRACO was agency solely responsible for the distribution and employment of all personnel who were assigned traffic functions. Telephone lines were laid by a signals unit with the advance guard along the route of the division commander. In addition to the trunk line, the German commanders would communicate using radios and messengers.

Air defense became increasingly important as the Luftwaffe lost its strength. To cope with the air threat, night marches and open columns kept the units dispersed. AA units were concentrated on key features—bridges, crossroads, and defiles.

Traffic Control[42]

The number of an armored division's *Feldgendarmerie* detachment who were trained in traffic control was around fifty officers and men, who had often been recruited from civilian police forces. Usually, these men would be under the command of the division operations officer, although a small number of men would be permanently assigned to the supply staff section. Both of these groups had broadly similar duties to one another, such as:

1. Post traffic information signs and mark out traffic routes.

2. Control traffic where necessary and, if the situation warrants it, reroute local traffic.

3. Control traffic at the division command post.

4. As with the Soviets, the Germans used barrier forces to ensure that there was no retreating without orders or absconding from the front line. The *Feldgendarmerie* supervised movements to the rear.

Of course, the MPs had other tasks such as undertaking patrols to maintain law and order during off-duty hours and guarding prisoners. Because of this, it was rare for the full detachment to be available for traffic control duties.

A traffic control post was normally composed of four MPs and a messenger and was equipped with two light personnel carriers and a motorcycle (although Kettenkrads and other transport were also employed). At full strength, from 12 to 15 traffic control posts could be established but when you take into account sickness, combat losses, furloughs, or other vacancies, in practice there were usually no more than six to eight.

In unusual situations or under extremely critical circumstances, traffic control elements of an MP battalion from a higher headquarters were sometimes placed at the disposal of an armored division in platoon or company strength for limited periods or within specific areas.

During the summer months, movements of armor proceeded with relative smoothness, and the normal complement of traffic control elements of the *Feldgendarmerie* detachment usually could cope with most of the traffic problems. In most instances it was merely necessary to strengthen the traffic control units in proportion to the distances involved. At times, however, considerable difficulty was faced when a series of downpours would suddenly convert the loamy soil of Ukraine into impassable quagmires. With the advent of fall and during the winter months that followed, entirely different conditions prevailed and could lead to insurmountable difficulties.

River Crossings[43]

Unit commanders were responsible for traffic control during river crossings. Thus, when a crossing was to be conducted within the boundaries of an armored division, the command staff of the division prepared and issued the necessary march and traffic orders to unit commanders and traffic control elements. They also designated the elements that (initially)

Two PzKpfw II Ausf As or Bs on a ferry made from two 8-ton *Bruckengerät B* sections—the *Brüko B* could make 8-ton bridges (pontoon trestle bridges) up to 83 m in length, 16 ton bridges to 54 m, and 4-ton/8-ton/16-ton ferries. This combination could carry 18-ton wheeled and 20–24-ton tracked vehicles (heavier because their footprint was reduced by tracks)—this was fine for early armor, but it wouldn't take a Panther. (NAC)

were to remain behind, the types and weights of the vehicles to be used, the concentration and dispersal areas on the bank of departure, and the holding areas, barrier lines, and assembly areas on the bank of arrival.

The main traffic control effort for river crossings changed as the operation progressed. At first it centered on the shore of departure, ensuring that traffic didn't obstruct the bridge-building troops, but after the crossing began, the emphasis then became the bridge points themselves, which were all too easily blocked by enemy action, breakdowns, or just sheer bad driving. The key area of importance then shifted to the far bank, where unknown obstacles awaited, minefields being the trickiest potential problem. The important thing was to move forward and not to stop or hold up the advance.

German Tank Maintenance in World War II[44]

When the war began, the Panzerwaffe had a centralized maintenance system. Minor repairs were made in the field; more serious damage saw vehicles returned to their factory of origin.

This system worked well during the Polish campaign. After the fighting, the divisions returned to their peacetime garrisons where the vehicles were quickly repaired at depot maintenance installations and tank production plants. The same was true for the assault on the West. A large spare-parts depot for tanks was established in northern France, but as the fighting only lasted for six weeks, there were few problems. When hostilities ended, most of the armored divisions returned to Germany—and those that didn't made use of the former French Army repair shops.

After the short campaigns in the Balkans in spring 1941, the armored divisions were rehabilitated in the zone of the interior and transferred to assembly areas for the campaign against Russia.

It was in North Africa that problems appeared. Transport difficulties and distance from Germany meant that a rigidly centralized maintenance system was not feasible. There was a greater emphasis on field maintenance, but that depended on a flow of supplies, and when the German Army became more heavily engaged in Russia, the supply situation in Africa became problematic.

For *Barbarossa*, the Germans had also intended to deal with major maintenance in the zone of interior, but had also provided each of the three army groups with a spare-parts depot. However, planning fell short. Buoyed up by their successes, the Germans expected military operations to be over before the winter.

How wrong can you be?

German tank losses in Russia were far heavier than they'd been during the earlier campaigns due to both

Opposite: Everything seemed heavy when it came to the Tigers: here a Kfz 100 Bussing-Nag 4500A with a Bilstein 3-ton crane is lifting, moving, or replacing a Tiger drive-sprocket. There are a lot of onlookers: too many "experts" and not enough workers! (GF Collection)

This page: Tanks need to travel—and if possible, they need to be transported rather than use their own temperamental engines and tracks. The most obvious method of long-distance travel in Europe is railroads—and they were used extensively for men, supplies, and vehicles. There was one problem: size, as exemplified by the Tiger. The width of its tracks (725 mm) made the vehicle too wide to be safely transported by rail (**above left**). There was a solution. The tracks were removed, as were the outside wheels, and narrower tracks were substituted—as is happening (**center left**) to A23, a Tiger of III./Panzerregiment Großdeutschland being readied for a rail flatbed car in mid-1944. (NARA; GF Collection)

Left: Overcomplicated? The drawbacks of the interleaved-wheel layout (*Schachtellaufwerk*) were the complexity of maintenance and repair in the field. However, it provided better weight distribution, reduced ground pressure, and enhanced maneuverability. (See also p. 70.) (NARA)

Above left: A Panther Ausf G undergoes a transmission change courtesy of an SdKfz 9 Famo recovery vehicle (a Famo with a boom and winch). Note the clevis (**A**) attached to left-hand side of hull. These practical items of equipment allowed a vehicle to be easily attached to tow. (Bundesarchiv Bild 101I-280-1096-33)

Above right: Unloading a PzKpfw III Ausf J from a rail flatbed car, Moscow area, November 1941. Its camouflage has been crudely applied in this first—and coldest—of the four Eastern Front winters. (NAC)

Below: When circumstances allowed, engines were airlifted because of the huge distances involved when fighting in Russia, and because of the desperate need for them at the front. The need for spares was chronic and continued until the end of the war. The mode of transport is the "*Tante-Ju*"—the Ju 52. The paucity of German transport aircraft was exacerbated by attrition during the Stalingrad campaign. The German aviation industry just didn't build enough of them (fewer than 5,000; the Americans built twice as many C-47 Skytrains); they flew too slowly to be able to evade enemy fighters; and they couldn't carry very much. (NARA)

J. S. Fries & Son of Frankfurt manufactured a portable gantry crane with a capacity of 15,000 kg (33,000 lb). It was used by field tank-maintenance units to remove turrets and engines from heavy German tanks. (NARA)

enemy action and mechanical problems caused by the great distances which had to be travelled and the weather conditions. Tank maintenance services weren't helped by a lack of local facilities and inadequate road and rail networks, with the latter's infrastructure crippled by demolitions carried out by the retreating Soviets as well as the fact that they spirited most of the locos and rolling stock away from the Germans. With so many transport problems the centralized system of maintenance was no longer practical and so maintenance became decentralized and took place in the field rather than at home.

To accomplish this, a range of measures were taken:

a. The strength of the maintenance units in the field was considerably increased and replacements were given better technical training.

b. Improved equipment and more efficient recovery vehicles were made available. Some new special-purpose equipment was developed.[45]

c. New depot maintenance installations were established in the Russian theater to take over those repair functions that formerly had been performed in Germany.

d. The manufacture of spare parts in Germany was stepped up to meet the increased demands of units in the field.

e. The parts supply organization was radically changed in order to afford a more rapid and efficient distribution of spare parts.

f. Qualified officers were given specialized tank-maintenance training before being assigned to commands in the field and to technical staff positions.

g. Certain functions hitherto accomplished by top-level agencies in the zone of interior were transferred to headquarters in the field.[46]

It wasn't until the summer of 1942 that these changes took effect, and by then there were other problems—first and foremost being a lack of spare parts, a problem exacerbated by the huge range of equipment within the Wehrmacht's inventory. With its limited industrial capacity, Germany was unable to produce new tanks and a satisfactory amount of spare parts at the same time.

In May 1942, the Ministry of Armaments decided to reduce new tank production and increase the output of spare parts. This didn't work. The German summer offensive in 1942 saw more than 75 percent of the Wehrmacht's total tank strength employed. Battle and other damage saw hundreds of tanks disabled, and these tanks couldn't be repaired because the spare parts weren't available. This affected German offensive power; for instance, the introduction of new Tiger tanks in the fall 1942 ran into problems. Spare parts for the new heavy tanks were few and far between—only one spare engine and one spare transmission were produced for every 10 tanks. Most of the Tigers were soon put out of action because of a lack of parts.

The introduction of the Panther in 1943 also led to problems. Insufficient testing meant that design and construction issues—particularly steering—saw all 325 Panthers withdrawn from the front and returned to the zone of interior for rebuilding. A special tank-repair plant was established near Berlin, but as the initial deficiencies were corrected, it became apparent that the engine was proving inadequate. It wasn't until fall 1943 that a decent engine became available. The Panther arrived too late to play a significant role when the Germans needed it.

Spare parts were a problem right to the end of the war, but this wasn't the only maintenance problem for the Panzerwaffe: slipping training standards had a big impact. Training methods changed as the 12-week-long program used by the tank-training companies of the *Ersatzheer* (replacement army) in the early war was shortened because casualties meant replacements were required at the front. The training was initially only for tank drivers and organizational maintenance personnel, but that soon changed to include a range of add-on courses upon completion of basic training for other maintenance personnel. In time, a six-week specialized training course was provided at *Wehrkreis* level, but this was found to be too short, particularly when the spare-parts problems, climate, and distances involved in the North African and Soviet theaters increased the need for improvisation and working around problems. Advanced training was provided at the depot maintenance installations where trainees undertook repair work supervised by civilian technicians and expert mechanics. This gave them practical experience before they joined a tank maintenance unit in the field. Unfortunately, as the war continued, abbreviated training schedules and unavailability of spare parts saw many recoverable vehicles destroyed by their crews rather than surviving to fight again.

There was some improvement in 1944–45 as German retreats brought the front lines closer to the depots and factories in Germany, were it not for the fact that so many of these buildings were lost to Allied bombing.

Winterketten and *Ostketten*[47]

All tank crews found the snow and wintry conditions hard going. First, the extreme cold led to innumerable problems as lubricants froze. When the crew did get the Panzers moving, snow and ice wedged into tracks and wheels. The experience of the winter of 1941/42 led to the development of *Winterketten* (winter tracks), that extended outwards to give a greater track width and, therefore, more floatation. They used the same track pin but were wider—they were nearly 600 mm wide, as compared to the more usual PzKpfw III and IV tracks that were 380 mm or 400 mm.

The *Winterketten* worked—to a point. There were problems with track breakages and transmissions, and they tended to snap when they encountered something solid. They also couldn't be used with *Schürzen* (side skirts).

In 1944, another track link was developed to try and deal with the impassable muddy conditions of the *rasputitsa*—the period in fall and spring when rain and snow/ice thaw

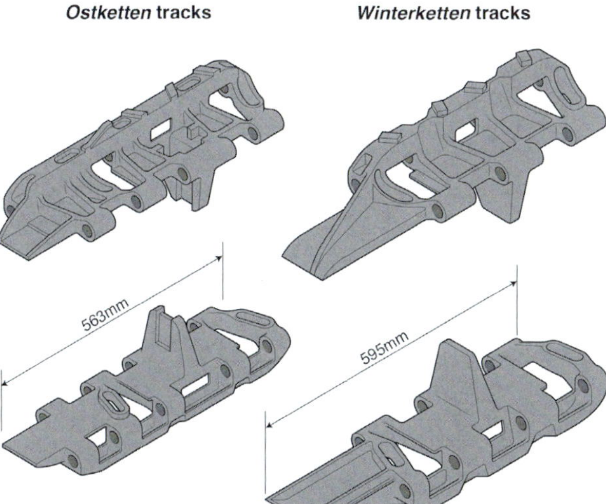

PzKpfw IV Ausf G 401 of Panzerregiment 27 (19. Panzerdivision) in February 1943. It has *Winterketten*—note the length of the blades. There were many different types and sizes of tracks, including the special wider *Ostketten* on the PzKpfw IV which were 560 mm wide (as compared to 400 mm). All tracks were given a KGS number where K = *Schnelllauffähige Kette für Kraftfahrzeuge* (high-speed tracks for motor vehicles); g = *Stahlguß aller Legierungen* (cast steel alloy); s = *schwimmende Bolzen* (floating pin). (GF Collection)

turned the roads of Eastern Europe into rivers of mud, especially in Ukraine. At around 560 mm wide, this new link, the *Ostketten* (literally, East tracks), wasn't as wide as the *Winterketten*, though it too used the normal track pin. The *Ostketten* was less likely to snap, could be used with *Schürzen*, and proved better than the *Winterketten* in mud as it accumulated less detritus—but it didn't stop the Panzers from getting bogged down.

These tracks were used by PzKpfw IIIs, IVs, and other variants using the same chassis. An ice cleat was developed for the Tiger I for the winter of 1943/44. These *Mitstollen* were supposed to be installed on every fifth or seventh cleat. They wore out after 30–40 km of use, and it's unclear whether they were made available or used in quantity by Tiger I or II.[48]

| Tactics

The Germans' professional approach to war and the battlefield was based on a simple concept: initiative. The word that tends to be most often associated with this is *Auftragstaktik*, usually translated as mission-based tactics as opposed to *Befehlstaktik*, the order-based approach that saw commanders give detailed and specific orders to their subordinates and so on down the chain of command, the bottom layers of which were just supposed to follow orders.

Mission-based tactics meant that commanders gave orders to their subordinates without minute levels of detail. Commands expected subordinates to come up with the best method of achieving the goal, and even allowed them the latitude to change the goal itself if the spirit and circumstances led to another, better option.

This is not to say that junior officers could do what they liked. They had to work within a sensible military framework, and they had a duty to do what their commander wanted. However, this approach meant that NCOs and even ordinary soldiers were expected to show a sensible amount of initiative—always remembering that there might be consequences if the goal wasn't achieved. German training, particularly with large formations, made allowances for this and would have approved of the tactics employed by Patton in the Louisiana Maneuvers of 1941.

One of the most important tenets of *Auftragstaktik* to the German Army was that commanders of units in the field—especially divisional commanders—should be in the

Weighing in at just over 18 tons, this Panzerregiment 36 PzBefWg III proved too much for a very basic wooden bridge over the Khorol River near Zubani, Ukraine, on September 14, 1941. Note the large frame antenna and, on the rear right hull, the NKAV— *Nebelkerzenabwurfvorrichtung*—smoke grenade dispenser. Not visible is the dummy 3.7 cm gun which this vehicle would have mounted, clearing the turret for command maps, etc. The regiment, part of 14. Panzerdivision, was destroyed at Stalingrad. (Bundesarchiv, Bild 146-1975-078-25A/Plessen, von [CC-BY-SA 3.0])

The first of the command tanks was the *Kleiner Panzerbefehlswagen* based on the PzKpfw I Ausf B. which had two radios—the FuG6 and FuG2. It remained in service till 1942, when the III took over. (NARA)

thick of the battle, close enough so that they could have a real feel for what was going on and an idea of what they needed to do to accomplish their mission effectively.

During the war, as Hitler and the High Command became more involved in the details, many senior commanders felt that *Befehlstaktik* had taken over from *Auftragstaktik*. It's also worth pointing out that it can be argued that tactics were a strength of the German armed forces in both world wars but that they perhaps concentrated too much on this rather than strategy. Certainly, the mismanagement of the war on a strategic level—not helped by the labyrinthine politics of the Nazi Party, economic mismanagement, and the monolithic structure of military control exerted by Hitler—became patently obvious the longer it went on.

Command Vehicles

Every level of the army had its HQ and staff—from *Zug* to *Heeresgruppe*. In the main, these involved a commander and his assistant in two tanks with extra radios. The further up the chain of command you went, so the number of staff and radios increased. Guderian in 1940 was classically illustrated in the back of an SdKfz 251-6 that was filled with radios and, visible in some versions of the photograph, an Enigma encoding machine.

Often, it was obvious which of the vehicles were involved in command by their aerials, which meant that they were targeted, and the number of junior officers and NCOs killed while their heads were sticking out of their tanks, visible to the enemy, was substantial. On a wider scale, 136 German generals were killed in or died of wounds caused by action, including 110 divisional commanders.

Hauptmann Clemens-Heinrich Graf von Kageneck, commander of sPzAbt 503, having just received orders from an aircraft probably in the Belgorod area, 1943. His command Tiger, turret number I, has FuG8 (star) and FuG5 aerials. Note the turret pistol port. (GF Collection)

Panzer Vorwärts!—Aber mit Verstand

In the Foreword to this *Panzer Vorwärts!*, Generalinspekteur der Panzertruppen Heinz Guderian discussed tactical leadership:

> It has been shown time and again in Russia that—in contrast to the Bolsheviks—it's not the type or number of our tanks that matters, but the fighting spirit of our tankers; this is why our tanks have always been victorious.
>
> However, fighting spirit alone cannot guarantee success; neither can armament, speed, and armor, nor the number of tanks, if the Panzer commander cannot lead and use his tanks correctly.
>
> In combat, the essential prerequisite for any success is the quality of tactical leadership, especially as we want to achieve that success with few or, even better, without any losses.

He continued by outlining key fighting principles "to provide the young officer who is yet to have experienced combat not only with examples of previous battles but also to analyze them in a clear and unambiguous form."

- Make sure you know the lie of the land. Prepare by studying the maps and any information you can get from other units. Make sure you share the information with your subordinates. Knowledge of the terrain is key to any attack. Getting this right will make the difference between victory and defeat.
- Always make time to make sure your subordinates understand the tactical position, mission, and anything that may have an impact on the forthcoming action. If you rush and omit this step, losses will be on your head and may impact the mission.
- *AUGEN AM FEIND*! Always keep your eye out for the enemy! Careful reconnaissance will stop unwelcome surprises. Watch your flanks!
- In combat, always be aware of the changing situation. You can't make the right command decisions if you don't know what's going on. You must be ready to issue short, clear and timely orders.
- Maintain strict radio silence unless there's an emergency. Leave the net clear for the unit commander.
- Ensure you lead with strength—at least two tanks up—and that trailing platoons are close enough to provide support when it's needed. The more fire you can lay down when you get into a fight, and the faster you react, the fewer casualties you'll take.
- Break cover as a unit and with speed. The more targets the enemy has, the more difficult it will be for him to choose the best ones and the more firepower you'll be able to lay down.
- There are only two speeds in combat: firing speed and flat out. Going slowly just makes it easier for an enemy to target you.
- If the antitank fire is from close range, don't stop. Attack at top speed with all weapons firing.

- Never let a single platoon attack antitank weapons, even when protected by powerful covering fire. In Russia, lone tanks are dead tanks! Antitank weapons are never deployed on their own.
- Don't bunch! Keep your distances between vehicles to complicate the enemy's firing options.
- Don't waste time thinking if you are faced with an impassable obstacle such as a minefield or antitank ditch. Immediately give the order to withdraw before you sustain losses. Do your thinking in cover.
- Think carefully before you pass a potential enemy position—such as a treeline. Either get close enough to be inside their minimum range or far enough away to be outside their range altogether.
- Don't attack enemy tanks head on. If they see you, they can hit you before you hit them. Move into better firing positions, surprise them from flank or rear. If you repel an enemy attack, pursue the retreating foe aggressively.
- If you're static, always dig in and camouflage well. It's no use being sorry after you've taken casualties from air or artillery attack.
- When you need to lay down heavy fire, if a critical moment arrives—such as an emergency attack—don't worry about conserving ammunition.
- Don't split your force and fight in two places unsupported: concentrate your power against objectives one by one. You'll achieve your mission with fewer casualties.
- Never misuse attached units. Don't use Panzergrenadiers as Panzers, engineers as infantry, or tank destroyers as assault guns.
- Attached units under your command aren't servants but guests! You are responsible for supplying them. Don't just use them as guards. They'll do their job better when you need them—and that will be often.
- Combined operations are just that. Stick together. Don't be separated. The enemy will try to do that but your watchword must be "Protect the infantry," just as theirs should be "Protect the Panzers."
- Stick to the mission. Don't get sidetracked unless an enemy is compromising your mission. If he is, take him out.
- After a victory don't rest on your laurels! Keep your helmets on. Prepare for the inevitable counterattack, which may come from an unexpected direction. You can enjoy your victory later.
- Tanks are best used aggressively in defense. Don't tie them down and simply make use of their firepower. Use only a few defensively and keep the remainder under cover as a mobile reserve.
- Never forget that your men belong to Germany not you. Going after personal glory only works once in a blue moon and usually leads to casualties. Against the Soviets let your head rule: concentrate on your strengths—cunning, tactical ability, and training. That way you'll achieve success and your men will respect you and follow you.
- In the past, the cavalry ruled the battlefield: today, it's the Panzer. And *Panzertruppen* must be as aggressive as the cavalry used to be. Remember Blücher's motto: "Forward and through! (But with intelligence)."

PzBefWg III of Panzerregiment 8's CO, Oberstlt Hans Cramer. Note palm tree insignia on the uparmored hull front, turret R (in red) and regimental command pennant, British ammo box on left fender and the range of clothing: it gets cold at night in the desert. Based on the Ausf H, this has a frame antenna, fixed turret, and fake gun. (NARA)

Tank Attack

The U.S. Army's 1945 *Handbook on German Military Forces*[50] gave a considered judgement on German Panzer tactics, identifying the fundamental principle of their offensive doctrine was to encircle and destroy the enemy, to bring armored forces and infantry into decisive action with sufficient firepower and shock. Superiority in force and firepower, as well as the surprise element, played a significant part. Coordination between the combined arms was essential if these shock tactics were to succeed. They concentrated their forces at a point of main effort (*Schwerpunkt*) for a breakthrough, allotting narrow sectors of attack (*Gefechtsstreifen*) to the troops committed.

Most of the German wartime successes were achieved with armored formations, and while the types of attack changed during the war, the fundamental theory stayed the same. However, the late-war dominance of the air by the Allies led to greater tank–infantry coordination. They had learnt at heavy cost—and, conversely, by beating off British attacks in the desert—the futility of charging a hostile antitank defense with tank concentrations. As the Soviet skills increased, the Germans learnt that large formations of tanks cannot achieve a breakthrough opposed by an effective screen of antitank guns without the assistance of other arms. Therefore, attention was given to the combined tactics of tanks and Panzergrenadiers.

Great emphasis in German offensive theory was laid on the role of the artillery, although in practice the artillery support role devolved to an ever-increasing degree on the tanks and assault guns. The Germans tended to detach field artillery battalions from their field artillery regiment and replaced the massed artillery fire with the fire of multi-barreled mortars and rocket projectors, though these latter hadn't the accuracy of the former.

When the enemy had well-prepared positions with natural or constructed tank obstacles, the German infantry attacked before the tanks

In various circumstances, hand signals—or lights at night—were used: when radio silence was in force; if the commander thought the radio net had been compromised; recce troops near an enemy; or during a silent advance. The key to any form of signals is that everyone understands what they mean. The Germans trained extensively with hand signals. They (and light signals) were standardized in Army Service Regulations—*Heeresdienstvorschrift*—472. (NARA)

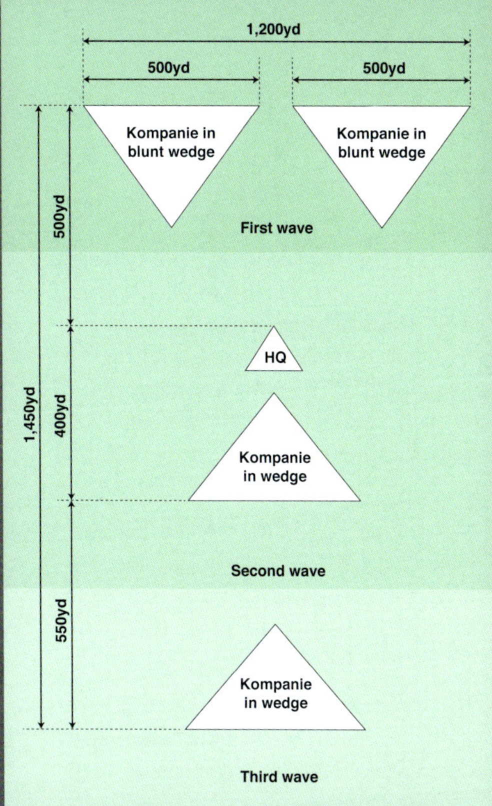

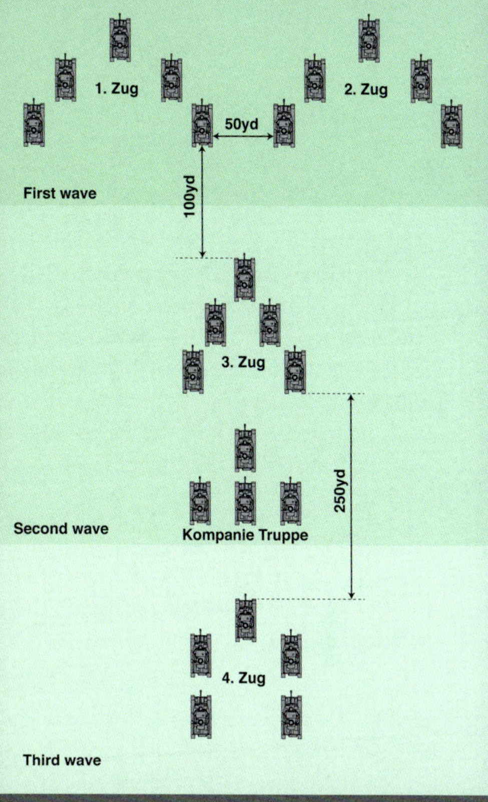

Attack by Motorized Forces

The basic formation for the tank platoon (*Zug*), company (*Kompanie*), and battalion (*Abteilung*) were file, double file, wedge, and blunt wedge—depending largely on the terrain and the strength of opposition. A Zug normally consisted of a tank and two tank squads of two tanks each. The tank regiment normally attacked in waves, usually echeloned in depth, one Abteilung following the other. The regimental commander's location was between the two Abteilungen. The normal depth of such a formation was about 2,745 m (3,000 yds). The attack normally proceeded in three waves. The first wave thrust to the enemy's antitank defense and artillery positions. The second wave provided covering fire for the first wave, and then attacked the enemy's infantry positions, preceded, accompanied, or followed by part of the Panzergrenadiers, who dismounted as close as possible to the point where they could engage the enemy.

The objectives of the second wave were the remaining antitank positions, positions of heavy infantry support weapons, and machine-gun emplacements holding up the advance of the infantry. The third wave, accompanied by the remainder of the Panzergrenadiers, mopped up. Sometimes three waves were telescoped into two, the first wave speeding through the enemy's position as far as his gun positions, the second crushing the enemy's forward positions in detail and mopping up the opposition not dealt with by the first wave, or which had revived since the first wave had passed through. The artillery FOO traveled in his armored vehicle with the first wave, while the artillery commander of the supporting artillery units traveled with the tank commander. Assault guns normally also accompanied the second wave. The tanks helped each other forward by fire and movement, medium or heavy tanks taking up hull-down firing positions and giving covering fire while the faster tanks advanced to the next commanding feature. Then the latter gave covering fire to the former, moving forward to their next bound. (After U.S. Army TM-E 30-451)

and cleared the way. The objective of the infantry was to penetrate the enemy position and destroy enemy antitank weapons. It would do so as much as its strength and the firepower of its own support weapons allowed, augmented by additional support and covering fire from the tanks and self-propelled weapons sited in their rear. Only after the destruction of the enemy antitank defense could the tanks be employed on the battle line to the fullest advantage. When the tank obstacles in front of the enemy position were already destroyed, and no additional tank obstacles were expected, the infantry would break through simultaneously with the tank unit.

In most cases, the infantry followed the tanks closely, taking advantage of the firepower and paralyzing effect of the tanks upon the enemy's defense. The Germans normally transported the infantry to the line of departure on tanks or troop-carrying vehicles to protect them and to increase speed. The infantry left the vehicles at the last possible moment and went into action mainly with light automatic weapons.

The tanks advanced by bounds from cover to cover, reconnoitering the terrain ahead and providing protective fire for the dismounted Panzergrenadiers. The tanks didn't slow their advance to enable the infantry to keep continuous pace with them, but advanced alone and waited under cover until the infantry caught up. Terrain that didn't offer sufficient cover was crossed with the greatest possible speed.

When a tank company attacked with infantry, there were normally two platoons on the line, one platoon back, and the fourth platoon in reserve. The interval between tanks was usually 90–110 m (100–120 yds). The tanks' machine guns usually engaged infantry targets at about 900 m (1,000 yds) range and under, while the tank guns engaged targets at 1,800–2,300 m (2,000–2,500 yds). The coordination between tanks and Panzergrenadiers moving into combat on armored halftracks was similar to the technique employed in a purely armored formation, since the armored halftracks were not only troop-carrying vehicles but also combat vehicles.

When the terrain was favorable for tank warfare, the Panzergrenadiers in their armored halftracks followed immediately with the second wave after the first tank wave overran the opponent's position. A deep and narrow formation was employed. After the penetration, the main mission of the Panzergrenadiers was to overcome the enemy positions which survived the first wave.

Tanks in Withdrawal

Experience showed that in certain types of terrain a reinforced rearguard company could hold up very superior forces on a front as wide as three miles. In one instance of a withdrawal from a defensive position along a river line, a German Panzer division, which had one Panzergrenadier battalion and attached elements as its rearguard, was covered by one rifle company reinforced by a company of tanks, four infantry guns (including two self-propelled), and a battery of medium howitzers. The tanks were mainly used to cover the withdrawal of the rifle elements. On another occasion a similar rear party had several heavy mortars attached. These covered the infantry withdrawal with the help of four tanks, which also carried the mortars back to the next bound.

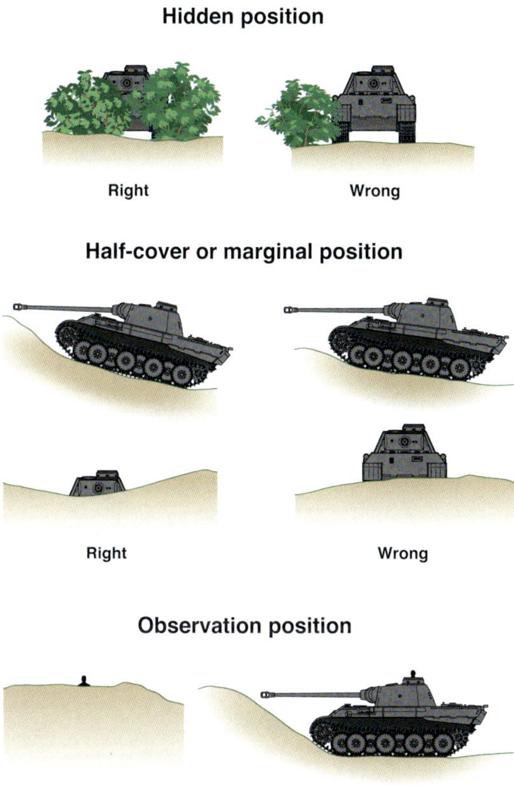

Not what Panzers liked doing, but in defense there were occasions when they had to be dug in. Key elements were to be properly hull-down so that their silhouette didn't give the position away. The tank also had to be able to leave the position safely and move to another without being seen. Here, a PzKpfw IV Ausf F1 with a 7.5 cm KwK L/24 gun next to a low-profile bunker in April snow, 1942. Note the MG 34 and spotter. (NAC)

The armored reconnaissance battalion of the Panzer division was particularly suited for rearguard tasks because of its armor and high firepower. When employing the armored reconnaissance battalion in terrain that afforded cover, the Germans sited well-camouflaged, armored halftracks in wooded areas, flat reverse slopes, or high grain fields, and opened fire with all weapons at very close range. The armored halftracks then penetrated the confused enemy and, after repulsing him, retreated to previously organized alternate positions.

Delaying actions were organized not in a main defensive belt, but on lines of resistance. The distance between such lines should be great enough to prevent the enemy from engaging two of them from the same artillery position: he should be compelled to displace and move up his artillery to engage each line. These lines of resistance were normally established along forward slopes to facilitate disengagement and withdrawal under cover. The delaying actions were fought forward of the lines of resistance with mobile forces. Furthermore, battle outposts were organized forward of each line. The main delaying weapons were machine guns, mortars, and self-propelled weapons. Tanks were used in small groups.

Maintenance of contact was a most conspicuous principle in the Germans' conduct of a withdrawal and delaying action—that way the size, composition, direction, and intention of the attacking enemy force were always observed.

Life in the Field

It's difficult for the outsider to understand what life as a member of a tank crew was like. In combat, the smallest mistake could lead to death. While the commander was in charge, and his orders had to be followed immediately and without hesitation in action, out of combat there were fewer distinctions—although that didn't always go down well with the powers that be, as Sander related:

> I have been ordered to inform my crews, immediately and without delay, that they must always salute me, except when in battle. Discipline in my gang has become too lackadaisical … And when I step outside, there are Tutasz, Oberholz and Turonski, the youngest man of the company, taking the piss out of me and practicing "saluting" … I did have to laugh about the three ugly bastards.
>
> While each of the men had their own duties, basic maintenance was the responsibility of everyone in a good tank crew: filling up with POL (petroleum, oil, and lubricants) checking the brake system and lighting, track maintenance—whenever and wherever, it was always better to repair or replace and correct track tension, etc., before a problem could render the vehicle unserviceable—loading with ammunition, barrel rodding, and all the other housekeeping and general cleaning duties. One tank commander wrote that his driver, Eschrich, "would rather have us take our boots off in case we broke anything."

This section and following images give a brief photographic treatment to the subject but is curtailed by reason of space. I recommend Schneider (2006 and 2016) and Sander (2022) for lengthier treatments.

There's always something to clean and lubricate on a tank. Here, a PzKpfw III Ausf H's 5 cm KwK L/42 barrel is cleaned in the North African desert. Note the shrouding around the base, the MG barrel, and the added frontal armor. The man shown at the top seems to be cleaning the coaxial MG prior to masking it. Crews had to be fully acclimatized to work topless. In most armies, getting sunburned was a chargeable offence! (GF Collection)

Above: 21. Panzerdivision in France, summer 1944: the crew of a PzKpfw IV Ausf H or J enjoy a break—and a cigar. Note the cans of food in the box on the glacis. Much of the food came in cans (e.g., the anonymous *Fleischkonserve*—canned meat), as did condensed milk and soups, although the most famous German ration since introduced in the Franco-Prussian War of 1870 was the *Erbswurst* (pea sausage) soup, so called because the concentrate was originally in a wrapped sausage shape. Various other ration packs existed, including the 2 *Tagessätze Zusatzverpflegung für Panzerkampfwagen Besatzungen* (two daily portions of additional food for tank crews) that came in a cardboard box and contained boiled sweets, *Scho-Ka-Koka*—chocolate with a high caffeine content—and fruit bars. These provided energy when crews needed a lift in combat. (NAC)

Above right: On top of the road wheels was as good a place as any to grab a nap if the opportunity arose—if a bit muddy. Lack of adequate sleep was a constant concern, and was not helped by Pervitin, the methamphetamine that saw extensive use during the war—particularly in 1940, when German soldiers were given tablets to help them stay awake during the battle for France. Later it was also used in the East, even after it had been officially banned in Germany in 1941. (NARA)

Center right: The majority of fiddly jobs are more difficult in winter when it's cold. Here, crew are checking that the MG rounds are correctly fitted to the links as they belt up MG ammunition atop a PzKpfw IV. (NAC)

Right: Panzer crew in winter gear taking the opportunity to have a meal at the front of Tiger 332 of sPzAbt 501 in early 1944—a long way from the North African desert, where the first version of sPzAbt 501 fought and entered captivity. (Bundesarchiv, Bild 101I-277-0846-08/Jacob [CC-BY-SA 3.0])

| Conclusion

For too long the Western view of World War II has held sway. This view has been warped by various factors: first and foremost, anti-communist views quickly saw the Soviet Union move from ally to enemy. This, in turn, meant that NATO needed what was then West Germany to play a significant role. Suddenly, almost overnight, the world order had changed and the Bundeswehr—many of whose officers had fought for their country in 1945—stood shoulder to shoulder with people they had fought against. So, the second factor: the rehabilitation of the Wehrmacht became part of the story. The narrative about the German armed forces changed to promote the idea of a clean Wehrmacht, that had nothing to do with Nazis or Einsatzgruppen, who could be seen as honorable men who had fought for their country, not the regime.

This was rubbish, of course, as were the attempts to whitewash the Waffen-SS, but the West was happy to believe them and preferred to propagandize Red Army atrocities to create sufficient resolve to accept a tainted bedfellow.

The third factor was the insistent promotion of the idea that it was numbers that had defeated the Germans, although the increasingly mad decision-making of an aberrant leader hadn't helped.

These factors helped ensure that the new generation was made up of fans who worshipped the "Big Cats"—the Panthers and Tigers—as the acme of the tank designer's art, who took it as gospel that the German soldier was head and shoulders above all others, that the number of kills claimed by the Panzer commanders was accurate, and who rather fancied the Panzer black.

Today, there's a more nuanced view. The qualities and skills of the Allies are acknowledged, and the German view of the Eastern Front has been broadened by work in the Russian archives—although recent politics have once again closed the doors that had opened. Today, the skills of the Red Army are recognized as well as its numbers. There's an understanding that a more balanced view of the tank battles is needed and that some of the statistics quoted have been, at best, the equivalent of comparing apples with bananas, and at worst just plain inaccurate.

However, one thing hasn't changed, and that's the fact that the German Panzers were a key factor in the conquest the Germans made from 1936 when they reoccupied the Rhineland to 1942 when their armies threatened Cairo, Stalingrad, and the oilfields of the Caucasus. They had reached that point without Panthers or Tigers in their inventory, against armies that had tanks that were at least as good, if not better, and despite logistical problems that made the Western Allies' difficulties in 1944 look like a minor issue.

What had made the difference between the two sides? The training, skill sets, and tactics of the German Panzer crew and all the other elements that made up the all-arms team of Blitzkrieg: infantry, artillery, engineers, Luftwaffe. When one reads the biographies, diaries, and papers of the Germans who fought in the period 1939–42, one is struck by their commitment to the cause. Very few of them doubted what they were doing. Then there's the length of time they spent training; their undoubted skill, often in the face of stern and brave opponents; and of course the complete idiocy of the whole thing as young men on both sides died in their millions with little to show at the end.

After 1942, the stories of the Panzer crews are those of survival in the face of extreme odds as they faced the whirlwind their attacks had stoked up. The Germans may have been wonderful tacticians endowed with amazing defensive qualities, but they were lousy strategists. Without the airpower to challenge the Allies, they were bombed and harried from the air and the sources of their raw materials were cut off. When the invasion of Normandy came, the Allies were hardly troubled by air or sea attacks, and it is noticeable that it was the Germans who developed most of the AA equipment of the war—and not just to stave off the strategic bombing campaign. While the success of the *Jabos* has been overstated, the men on the ground feared them and wanted AA defenses to keep them at bay.

After the great triumphs came great defeats. The training dropped off, the skills became less obvious. It's true that the German tanks of the later war years—the Tigers and Panthers—were a step up from the PzKpfw Is and IIs they had started with, but their enemies' weapons had also evolved—and the Allies had chosen to focus on furthering reliability and ease of manufacture to give them large numbers of tanks that withstood the pace of warfare better than the smaller numbers of cleverly engineered German vehicles. The *Panzertruppen* could do little but defend as best they could as the noose tightened. They fought for their mates because that's all they could do—and if they didn't, state retribution was final.

Above all, they hadn't stopped believing in the reasons why they went to war: over and over, the diaries evince the diarists' world weariness and the need to protect their families and homeland. There's a grudging respect for the Soviet resilience and for Allied industry, but the regrets they outline relate to not having struck the death blow, rather than having started the fight in the first place.

A Tigers of 3./sPzAbt 502 near Lake Ladoga. As two of the crew prepare for a swim, others clean boots, sort turret stowage boxes, and generally do the housekeeping. (GF Collection)

Notes

1. Sander, *Blood, Dust and Snow*. Entry for March 5, 1942.
2. Halder, *War Journal*.
3. Sander, *Blood, Dust and Snow*.
4. Liedtke, *Enduring the Whirlwind*.
5. Of an initial complement of 3,903 at the start of *Barbarossa*.
6. Of this number, Liedtke shows that few were operational—for example, on December 22, in HG Nord and Mitte, the 16 Panzer divisions had 1,185 Panzers, but only 405 were operational. Of the 2,345 noted here, over 1,015 were non-operational and more may have been in repair shops in Germany.
7. Liedtke points out an anomaly in the figures that leaves a huge number of German Army Panzers and StuGs—some two thousand—unaccounted for. Many could have been in repair shops; others could have been in the field but not properly accounted for.
8. Helped by the manufacture of nearly three thousand Panzers, German Army stocks of tanks stood at 4,524 on July 1, 1943, when the battle of Kursk began.
9. *www.dupuyinstitute.org/blog/2018/07/23/armor-exchange-ratios-at-kursk/*
10. The following tables are based on info in Jentz, Panzertruppen, Vol. 2. There were also 410 operational StuGs available. By March 15, 1945, this figure had shrunk to 67.
11. Much of the information here is based on two main sources: *www.lexikon-der-wehrmacht.de/Gliederungen/SchulenPanzer/Gliederung.htm* and Schools of the Wehrmacht: Schnelle Truppen—Panzertruppe: A project by Jan-Hendrik, Bernd R and Dmitrij2 garnered from *https://forum.axishistory.com/viewtopic.php?t=122616 and https://www.scribd.com/doc/52958690/Panzer-Schule*.
12. Ganz, *Ghost Division*.
13. Ashley Arensdorf, "British and German Approaches to Tactical Officer Training during the Late Interwar Period," from the *Military Review Online Exclusive* (December 2021).
14. Balck, *Order in Chaos*.
15. Radio info leans heavily on Komiya, *The Evolution of Headsets*.
16. Info from Michael Farnworth, *Introduction to German World War 2 Patterns*.
17. This is extremely well explained on the excellent Panzerworld website at *https://panzerworld.com/german-unit-strength-definitions*.
18. Wilbeck, *Sledgehammers*.
19. See *https://www.dasreich.ca/gnomestory.html*.
20. Paraphrased from Sander, *Blood, Dust and Snow*.
21. Zaloga, *Panzer 38(t)*.
22. Toppe, *Desert Warfare*.
23. Ibid.
24. von Senger und Etterlin, *German Tanks of World War II*.
25. *http://panzerivuniverse.phelpscomputerservices.com/Specs-02.htm*.
26. Womack, "Testing and Fielding of the Panther Tank."
27. Photo taken November 2013, at the Military Vehicle Technology Foundation, Jacques Littlefield Collection, Portola Valley, on San Francisco Peninsula.
28. Wilbeck, *Sledgehammers*.
29. Ibid.
30. Ibid.
31. Info from *https://panzerworld.com*.
32. *Handbuch Die Munition*.
33. Coox & Naisawald, *Survey of Allied Tank Casualties*.
34. Ibid. Landmines 20%, mechanical/terrain/non-enemy 13% (although this was given a proviso as being too low); hollow charge (Panzerfaust etc.) 7.5% (probably too high as not used outside Europe); miscellaneous/more than one type 5.5%. It's worth adding, however, that "Data on the repairability of tanks suggested the following percentages: mined tanks, 78 percent repairable; Panzerfaust weapons, 71 percent; and gunfire, 51 percent. Because of differing samples, no direct correlation could be established between the percentage burned and the percentage repairable."
35. Info from *https://panzerworld.com/* and Chamberlain & Doyle, *Encyclopedia of German Tanks*.
36. For what it's worth, *Tactical and Technical Trends*, No. 22, April 8, 1943, reported on the ammunition carried by two 5 cm armed PzKpfw IIIs in North Africa: "86 rounds were carried loose on the floor of Tank 1, and 83 in Tank 2. In the bins of the first tank were 92 rounds, and there was room for 7 additional rounds; in the bins of the second were 79 rounds with room for 17 more. This indicates a total stock of some 185 and 179 rounds per tank, respectively." The percentage splits in the two tanks were: Tank 1 45% HE, 55% AP; tank 2 32% HE, 68% AP. It's difficult to say quite how the loader or the turret traverse would have worked in such conditions.

Above: Crew stored personal gear, greatcoats, booty, and other essentials in the *Rommelkiste* or "rucksack" at the turret rear. This line of PzKpfw III Ausf Gs of 5. leichte Division is waiting to go to North Africa. (Fotocollectie Spaarnestad Onderwerpen/ Dutch National Archives)

Above Right: A Tiger of III./Panzerregiment Großdeutschland on a flatbed in Romania in 1944. Note the tent hanging from the gun barrel—somewhere for the crew to have a rest away from the elements on a long rail journey. (Bundesarchiv, Bild 101I-732-0133-34/Pfeiffer [CC-BY-SA 3.0])

Below: Card schools inevitably started whenever the chance arose, as it did here on a nice sunny day in Greece. As if by magic an accordion appeared as well—also good for morale. A PzKpfw III Ausf J lurks in the background of this *Signal* magazine image dated April 9, 1941. (GF Collection)

37. As a postscript, it appears that in some cases these screens may actually improve the efficiency of the hollow-charge weapons by helping the initiation of the plasma stream at the optimum point to penetrate the hull.
38. Quoted from *www.tankarchives.ca/2013/08/german-armour-quality.html.*
39. Jentz & Doyle, *Germany's Tiger Tanks.*
40. RAL = *Reichs-Ausschuß für Lieferbedingungen* = National Committee for Delivery conditions. Set up in 1925 as an independent organization to handle quality assurance, in 1927 it defined industry standards for 40 colors (today there are 2,328) and in 1938 produced the RAL 840 R catalogue with the original numbering system extended to four digits. Military colors were prefixed by 7 or 8. In 1942 the Third Reich issued a state ordinance and RAL lost its responsibility until it was reestablished postwar.
41. Toppe, *Desert Warfare.*
42. From Mueller-Hillebrand, *German Armored Traffic Control.*
43. Ibid.
44. This section leans heavily on Mueller-Hillebrand, *German Tank Maintenance.*
45. But never enough.
46. Mueller-Hillebrand, *German Tank Maintenance.*

47. See the excellent article at *http://panzerserra. blogspot.com/2020/05/panzer-iv-ausf-h-sdkfz-1612-with.html.*
48. Schneider, *Tigers in Combat III.*
49. These sections are edited quotations from TM-E 30-451.

References & Further Reading

Arensdorf, Ashley. "British and German Approaches to Tactical Officer Training during the Late Interwar Period" in *Military Review* online, December 2021.

Balck, Hermann. *Order in Chaos*. University of Kentucky Press, 2015.

Böttger, Armin. *To the Gate of Hell: The Memoir of a Panzer Crewman*. Frontline Books, 2012.

Chamberlain, Peter & Doyle, Hilary L. *Encyclopedia of German Tanks of World War II*. A&AP, 1978.

Coox, Alvin D. & Naisawald, L. van Loan. *Survey of Allied Tank Casualties in World War II*. The John Hopkins University Operations Research Office, 1951/52.

Davis, Brian L. *German Army Uniforms and Insignia 1933–1945*. Brockhampton Press, 1998.

ETHINT 38. Interview with Generaloberst Heinz Guderian, January 1948.

ETO Ordnance Technical Report No. 167. *Panther Recovery Tank*, NARA via Digital History Archive.

Farnworth, Michael. *Introduction to German World War 2 Patterns*. Accessed from www.artizandesigns.com/guides/germanpatterns.pdf

Ganz, A. Harding. *Ghost Division*. Stackpole, 2016.

German PzKw. III Tank: Report on Examination of the Turret and Armament. Dept of Tank Design, Ministry of Supply, August 1942.

German PzKw. IV Tank: Report on Examination of the Turret and Armament. Dept of Tank Design, Ministry of Supply, October 1943.

Halder, Franz. *War Journal*, Vol VII. Leavenworth, KS.

Handbuch Die Munition der deutschen Geschütze und Werfer. Berlin, 1943.

Jentz, Thomas L. *Panzertruppen*, Vol. 1 & 2. Schiffer, 1996.

Jentz, Thomas L. & Doyle, Hilary L. *Germany's Tiger Tanks VK45.02 to Tiger II: Design, Production and Modifications*. Schiffer, 1998.

Komiya, Nick. *The Evolution of Headsets and Throat Mikes for Panzers (1935–1945)*. Accessed from www.warrelics.eu/forum/field-equipment-accessories-third-reich/evolution-headsets-throat-mikes-panzers-1935-1945-a-618866/

Liedtke, Gregory. *Enduring the Whirlwind: The German Army and the Russo-German war 1941–1943*. Wolverhampton Military Studies No. 21, Helion, 2022.

Mueller-Hillebrand, Brig. Gen. Hermann Burkhart. *German Armored Traffic Control During the Russian Campaign*. Department of the Army Pamphlet 20-242, June 1952.

Mueller-Hillebrand, General Burkhart H. German Report Series: *German Tank Maintenance in World War II*. Department of the Army, 1954.

"Panzers across the Meuse" in *The Field Artillery Journal*, April 1941.

Report on Examination of German PzKw. IV Tank; Dept of Tank Design, Ministry of Supply, January 1942.

Report on PzKw. VI (Tiger) Model H Part II: Armament, Fighting Arrangements, Stowage and Power Traverse; Dept of Tank Design, Ministry of Supply, January 1944. NARA via Digital History Archive.

Richardson, Horst Fuchs. *Your Loyal and Loving Son: The Letters of Tank Gunner Karl Fuchs 1937–1944*. Brassey's Inc., 2003.

Sander, Friedrich. *Blood, Dust and Snow Diaries of a Panzer Commander in Germany and on the Eastern Front 1938–1943*. Greenhill Books, 2022.

Schneider, Wolfgang. *Panzer Tactics: German Small-Unit Armor Tactics in World War II*. Stackpole, 2006.

Schneider, Wolfgang. *Tigers in Combat I*. Stackpole, 2004.

Schneider, Wolfgang. *Tigers in Combat II*. Stackpole, 2005.

Schneider, Wolfgang. *Tigers in Combat III*. Helion, 2016.

Schnelle Truppen Teil 1 Panzer und Panzerjäger. Deutscher Volksverlag, 1940.

Tactical and Technical Trends, No. 22, April 8, 1943.

TM-E 30-451 *Handbook on German Military Forces*, 15 March 1945.

Toppe, Generalmajor Alfred. *Desert Warfare: German Experiences in World War II*. CSI Special Studies, Fort Leavenworth, 1991.

von Senger und Etterlin. F.M.: *German Tanks of World War II*. Arms & Armour Press, 1969.

Wilbeck, Christopher. *Sledgehammers Strengths and Flaws of the Tiger Tank Battalions in World War II*. Aberjona, 2004.

Williamson, Gordon. Warrior 46 *Panzer Crewman 1939–45*. Osprey, 2002.

Womack, John H. "Testing and Fielding of the Panther Tank and Lessons for Force XXI." U.S. Army Thesis, Defense Technical Information Center, 1977 accessed from https://apps.dtic.mil/sti/pdfs/ADA529493.pdf

Zaloga, Steven J. *Panzer 38(t)*. Osprey, 2014.

Websites

www.dasreich.ca/gnomestory.html

www.dupuyinstitute.org/blog/2018/07/23/armor-exchange-ratios-at-kursk/

https://forum.axishistory.com/viewtopic.php?t=122616

www.lexikon-der-wehrmacht.de/Gliederungen/SchulenPanzer/Gliederung.htm

https://panzerworld.com/

http://panzerivuniverse.phelpscomputerservices.com

www.scribd.com/doc/52958690/Panzer-Schule

Index